HUME'S THEORY OF THE UNDERSTANDING

HUME'S THEORY OF THE UNDERSTANDING

by

RALPH W. CHURCH

ARCHON BOOKS
1968

First published 1935
Reprinted 1968 in an unaltered
and unabridged edition
by permission of
George Allen & Unwin Ltd.

*This edition for sale only
in North and Spanish America*

Library of Congress Catalog Card Number: 68–11252
Printed in The United States of America

PREFACE

THE main interests of this essay, which has grown into its present form out of lectures delivered at Balliol College, Oxford, are indicated in the *Introduction*. Their relevance to matters that require further interpretation could hardly be made out by an apology for another book on Hume, and is to be found, if at all, in the course of the essay itself.

The extent of my indebtedness to Professor Laird's commentary, and to Professor N. Kemp Smith's papers on Hume (*Mind*, N.S. 14), is less evident than I could wish; and, for guidance in several connections, I am conscious of my debt to Professor Laing and Professor Hendel.

I wish to express my gratitude to Professor D. W. Prall for his generous criticism of the essay in manuscript form; to Miss Isabel P. Creed, to whom I am indebted in the matter of Hume's theory of abstract ideas; to Professor G. Watts Cunningham for several helpful suggestions; and to my mother, who kindly read the proof.

R. W. C.

ITHACA, NEW YORK
December II, 1934

CONTENTS

9

INTRODUCTION

IT is commonly suggested, as much by methods of exposition and what they ignore as by explicit statement, that Hume's philosophy is negative merely; and that this "total scepticism" derives exclusively from, and wholly depends upon, his views about impressions and ideas. Without those views, his scepticism would lack its premises. Therefore Hume is answered and disposed of simply by the fact that his major premise in method is crudely mistaken.

Yet even a moderately detailed examination of Hume's theories of causal inference and belief in substance may suffice to indicate how groundless is the charge of total scepticism, while at the same time it discloses the character of unanalysed experience in Hume's view. The relation between his critical analysis of causation and that of "the Cartesians," as well as the logical nature of Hume's arguments in that regard, make it plain that his analysis here is independent of his chief psychological dogma. And a brief consideration of Hume's theories of knowledge and belief with respect to the rationalism they would eliminate, and the sort of "atomism" which is held to be their self-stultifying vice, may suggest something of the character of Hume's positive theory of the understanding.

The several sections of Part I of Book I of the *Treatise* comprehend Hume's elucidation of what he says are "the elements of this philosophy." With the exception of mere fancies or "perfect ideas," these elements occur not in isolation, thereafter to be made into perceptions, but rather in the relationship that is the gentle force of association. This force of attraction is found in the three natural relations of resemblance, contiguity, and cause and effect.

"Natural relations" differ in a fundamental respect from relations of comparison, or "philosophical relations." The latter are cases of resemblance. Hume explains that "resemblance," like "being simple," is not a qualifying predicate. For, as the simplicity of a simple idea is not distinguishable from the idea itself, so in the case of perceptions resembling in a certain respect the resemblance is not distinguishable from the qualitatively identical but numerically repeated respect itself. Thus resemblance is not the proper name of any character or form in virtue of which resembling experiences are the same. On Hume's theory of abstract ideas, "resemblance" is a term verbal referring (in virtue of habits of association) to any case of a qualitative identity numerically distributed. And, since

12

Introduction

Hume does not use the term resemblance to name a form distinguishable from intrinsically resembling qualities, his denial of abstract general ideas is not inconsistent with his conception of resemblance as a philosophical relation.

Relations of comparison thus are not extrinsic connections at all. Did the theory of relations as philosophical exhaust Hume's conception of this one of the elements of his philosophy, the remaining elements would exist in no synthesis and be comparable merely. But natural relations, being "principles of union," or "cohesion," constitute the connecting factor in the perceptual situation. This is not to say that what is designated by "resemblance" is, in the natural relation thus distinguished, the connecting factor. So much as that would be the "philosophical" constituent only of the natural relation. The natural *and* connecting factor would be the gentle force that associates the (in certain respects) qualitatively identical experiences. Thus, in any case of the natural relation of resemblance there will be present intrinsically comparable impressions and ideas, *and* the factor of their association by the gentle force of attraction.

Hume's chief innovation in associationist theory is his inclusion of cause and effect among the natural relations, or modes of association. La Forge, Cordemoy, and Malebranche had antici-

13

pated Hume's critical analysis of causation without coming to this conclusion as to the nature of the causal relation; a fact which indicates at once that the conclusion itself is the result of Hume's own analysis of the matter, and that his analysis, in so far as it is merely sceptical, does not depend for its validity on his theory of impressions and ideas.

The constructive theory of causal inference, by which Hume connects his sceptical analysis of the causal relation with his final discovery of the impression of necessity in the felt determination of certain habits or customs in imagination, shows the limitations of such criticism as would dispose of Hume's conception of experience as atomistic merely. It will be recalled that Hume begins the *Treatise* with an analysis of "the perceptions of mind" into impressions and ideas; and that, in the subsequent sections of Part I, he discloses the remaining elements of perception. Therefore, it would be incorrect to identify perception with any one of its elements, or with all of them taken respectively in isolation. Only mere fancies or "perfect ideas" occur divorced from all associations. Normally, in the experience of mature persons, there occurs, at the least, a lively idea associated with a present impression; which is, by definition, the general nature of belief. These beliefs vary in elaborateness and force between the extremes of proof and mere chance; but only at the extreme of mere chance, or gratuitous fancy, do isolated impressions or ideas exist. Ordinarily, the terms of Hume's analysis of perception occur in the synthesis which he articulates in his theory of belief. Normal experience, then, will consist of perceptions, themselves the syntheses in habit which are beliefs.

Hume's account of the causes that induce us to believe in the continued and independent existence of perceived bodies, and his statement of the true idea of the self, supply a basis in theory on which the external world, in his view of it, may be distinguished from the self. The constant and coherent impressions and ideas which contribute to constitute the "systems" that are perceived bodies, are associated by the natural relation of resemblance. The operation of this relation is likewise integral to the felt continuity of the self, as Hume himself makes out that continuity. How, then, are the perceptions constituting the mind to be distinguished from those that are believed to be independent of the self, or "objective"? The perceptions of which the mind consists are to be distinguished in that they are associated not alone by resemblance, but also by the natural relation of cause and effect. This natural relation differs from those of resemblance and contiguity in being expectant or transitive in intent. Thus, within a belief in the continued and independent existence of a perceived body there is the association by resemblance of constant and coherent content, but no activity of transitive intent. A perceived body, therefore, will not be felt as expecting anything beyond itself. The true idea of the self, Hume says, is that of a system of perceptions related by cause and effect. The self, then, is a system of habits of causal inference, which differ from habits of belief in independent existence in that they alone are expectant or transitive. Thus, within experience, those perceptions which are felt as wholly actual and self-comprised are to be distinguished from those which are expectant; and those of the former kind will be the appearances of perceived bodies, while the latter are the habitual constituents of a self which is at once mnemonic and expectant.

In Hume's view, knowledge unqualified will consist in the awareness by direct comparison of the qualitative identities which cases of resemblance and degrees of quality are. Simple cases of proportion in quantity and number also may be thus directly given. But where the matter is at all complicated, requiring inference for its elucidation, we can only rely on habits of inference, the accuracy of whose activity is always doubtful.

This fact once recognized, and the fact that our faculties of inference are unable to attain certainty will be plain. Were it the nature of our understanding to be the "pure understanding" of Malebranche, divorced from imagination, and hence in no way influenced by habit or custom, the incompetence of apagogic reasoning in matters of fact, as well as the alogical nature of causal inference and of belief in the existence of bodies, would leave us no alternative but that of the total scepticism of the fantastic sect. Since, however, the understanding consists of habits of inference, it will be plain that nature determines us to infer, as she determines us to breathe and to feel. The general structure of these habits, formulated in rules by which to judge of causes and effects, is for Hume the logic of the actual understanding, itself consisting of habitually related beliefs or perceptions.

HUME'S THEORY OF THE UNDERSTANDING

CHAPTER I

"*The Elements of this Philosophy*"

I

HUME begins his analysis of the understanding by laying it down that, "All the perceptions of the human mind resolve themselves into two distinct kinds, which I shall call Impressions and Ideas."[1]* Perception is thus the genus of which impressions and ideas are the exhaustive species, differentiated by the superior force and vivacity of the former.[1] These "two species of perception"[4] are further to be divided into simple and complex impressions and ideas. Of these the simple are "such as admit of no distinction or separation"; the complex on the contrary consisting of parts, such as the colour, taste, and odour of an apple.[2] There is also a distinction to be made between simple and complex ideas. For since simple ideas differ from simple impressions only in force and vivacity, they will be more or less vivid copies of such impressions. But

* Where not otherwise indicated, references are to the Selby-Bigge edition of Hume's *Treatise*.

many complex ideas are not faithful copies of simple ideas compounded in fancy.

In his argument to show that all simple ideas are derived from impressions, Hume in effect makes out a difference between these two species of perception other than that of force and vivacity. For "by constant experience" he finds the simple impression to occur always before the corresponding idea. This is why a man born blind and deaf could have neither impressions nor ideas of colours and sounds.[5] The two exhaustive species of perception are thus differentiated both by the superior force and vivacity, and the priority in origin, of impressions. These two species are subdivided into complex and simple; a subdivision which brings out a third difference between simple ideas as representative and the simple impressions represented, themselves representative of nothing at all. The cause of the impressions of the senses is, in Hume's opinion, "perfectly inexplicable by human reason." Whether "they arise immediately from the object, or are produced by the creative power of the mind, or are derived from the author of our being," we cannot know.[84] Hence there is the further difference in kind between simple ideas and impressions; the one being representative, the other not.

That impressions "arise in the soul originally,

20

from unknown causes"[7] is true only of impressions of sensation, not of reflection. The latter are "derived in a great measure from our ideas. . . ."[7] When a "pleasure or pain of some kind or other"[8] is felt, it persists in idea, and this produces an impression of desire or aversion, hope or fear. And because this impression thus derives from an idea it is properly called an impression of reflection.[8] Although Hume here mentions as typical impressions of reflection "passions, desires, and emotions," the latter includes also the felt determination of the mind which is the functioning of custom or habit.[155, 156]

Since impressions of reflection are subsequent in time to those of sensation, and therefore "secondary" and derivative, why should they not be called ideas? Because impressions of reflection are "original facts and realities, complete in themselves, and implying no reference to other passions, volitions, and actions."[458] Again, Hume insists that "a passion is an original existence, and contains not any representative quality which renders it a copy of any other existence or modification."[415] Impressions of reflection are properly called impressions because they are not copies, but original existences, complete in themselves. Impressions of sensation are "original" in the double sense (*a*) that their occurrence is temporally prior to that of all other species of perception, and (*b*) that, involving no reference to anything beyond, they are complete in themselves. Though not original in the first sense, impressions of reflection are so in the second: like simple ideas, their causes are known; but unlike simple ideas they are self-contained, not representative. The characteristics common to all impressions will then be their superior force and vivacity, and their being self-contained. Impressions, then, are not expressions; for they refer to nothing beyond themselves.

The self-sufficiency of impressions is one characteristic of Hume's psychological atomism. The other characteristic he states as follows: "Whatever objects are different are distinguishable, and . . . whatever objects are distinguishable are separable by the thought and imagination."[18] This separateness of impressions and of ideas is first asserted in the concluding sentences of Section 3, *Of the ideas of memory and imagination*, or the faculties "by which we repeat our impressions."[8] Memories are repeated impressions which, in two respects, differ both from their prototypes and other ideas. In point of force and vivacity, a memory "is somewhat intermediate betwixt an impression and an idea";[8] and in point of the order of their recurrence, memories are "in a manner tied down"[9] to the order of the original impressions.

The other faculty by which impressions are repeated in idea is imagination, or fancy. Simple fancies will be copies of impressions; but copies which, having entirely lost the vivacity of memories, are "perfect" ideas.[8] Such ideas as these are "not restrained to the same order and form with the original impressions,"[9] but may be transposed and compounded at liberty by the fancy; a liberty which is to be explained by the fact that ideas are derived from impressions, of which no two are inseparable.[10] That is why, "Wherever the imagination perceives a difference among ideas, it can easily produce a separation."[10]

Hume refers the reader to his discussion, *Of the impressions of the senses and memory* (Part III, Sec. 5) for more light on the differences he finds between memories and fancies.[9] Yet here he virtually gives up the distinctions made in the earlier section. Though it be true that memory preserves the order and arrangement of the original impressions, in no given case can this be known to be so; "it being impossible to recall the past impressions, in order to compare them with our present ideas, and see whether their arrangement be exactly similar."[85] Hence the difference between memories and fancies is not actually to be found in the order of their complex ideas. Nor is that difference actually to be found in the nature of the simple ideas of memory and fancy. For these ideas are derived from impressions, which are neither mnemonic nor fugacious.[85] "Since therefore the memory is known, neither by the order of its *complex* ideas, nor the nature of its simple ones; it follows that the difference between it and the imagination lies in its superior force and vivacity."[85] There being no way in which the temporal order preserved by memory may be compared with the original impressions, the distinction between memories and fancies in point of temporal order can have no real significance. The difference between the one species[9] and the other can then be no more than "sensible"; a difference only in point of force and vivacity.*

But more than this, memories and fancies frequently cannot be distinguished in point of force and vivacity. Whenever memories lose their "lively colours" and become weak and feeble, we are frequently at a loss to decide whether they be other than fancies. And not even lively colours are a sure mark of memories. For if memories may fade, fancies may become obsessions; as in the case of liars "who by the frequent repetition of their lies," come to believe in them; "custom and habit having in this case,

---

* "A man may indulge his fancy in feigning any past scene of adventures; nor would there be any possibility of distinguishing this from a remembrance of like kind, were not the ideas of the imagination fainter and more obscure."[85]

as in many others, the same influence on the mind as nature, and infixing the idea with equal force and vigour."[86] In view of this power of the "second nature" that is custom, we shall later have to ask how Hume can distinguish sane beliefs from vested illusions.

The freedom of the fancy which, in Section 3 of Part I, is a known mark of its difference from memory, is a freedom to produce complex but not simple ideas. That every simple idea is derived from a corresponding impression, Hume at first "ventures to affirm"[3] is a rule without exception. Two pages over, however, he takes notice of "one contradictory phenomenon." Were a man confronted with every shade of a certain blue, except one which had never appeared in his experience, there could be little doubt of his ability to supply the deficiency by an act of imagination.

Mr. Whitehead has pointed out that this exception in the case of a hue must be extended to cover all cases of gradation in quality.* Hume's comparison here of sounds and colours in respect of gradation suggests that he so far anticipates this criticism.[5, 6] He also thinks "it may not be amiss to remark" here that there is "another limitation" to which the principle of the temporal priority of impressions is subject; viz. our power

* *Process and Reality*, p. 185.

to form "secondary ideas" which are copies of "primary" ideas, as the latter are copies of impressions.[6] And that such is the case, Hume says, "appears from this very reasoning concerning them."[6] But this is not so much an exception to the rule in question as an explanation of it. For if some ideas produce copies of themselves in secondary ideas, still these primary ideas derive from impressions. Hence it remains the case that simple ideas are copied "either mediately or immediately"[7] from impressions. Whether "this very reasoning"[6] which brings the fact of secondary ideas to light is about deficiencies in experience supplied by imagination, and not merely a reference to the subsequent "explanation" of the temporal priority of impressions, is not clear. But it is plain that an attempt to reconcile the contradictory phenomenon with Hume's copy theory of ideas could only fail. For, *ex hypothesi*, there is (and has been) no impression from which any idea, whether secondary or primary, might be derived.

Hume says of his analysis of perception into impressions and ideas that it "is the first principle I establish in the science of human nature; nor ought we to despise it because of the simplicity of its appearance."[7] For the question concerning the reality of innate ideas, which "has made so much noise in other terms," is simply a question as to the priority of impressions or ideas. If we examine the disputes of the philosophers in the matter of innate ideas, we shall find their arguments to prove precisely Hume's point that every idea is derived from a corresponding impression. This being realized, Hume hopes that his "clear stating of the question" will silence all dispute and make the principle of the origin of ideas of more use in explanation than has hitherto been the case.[7]

It is a commonplace that Hume's confidence in the importance for philosophy of his first principle is indefensible. Since images of memory cannot be distinguished with assurance from those of fancy, even in point of force and vivacity, and since imagination may "supply" ideas that are not copies, the only difference between impressions and ideas remaining is that of the temporal priority of the former. Yet, in his examination of the impressions of the senses and memory, Hume himself advances almost all that need be said in refutation of our alleged knowledge of this priority. For as no prototype of any memory may be revived, so no original of any primary idea may be recalled. In no case, then, can an idea be known to be a copy.

As for the difference between impressions and ideas in point of force and vivacity, "in a fever, in madness, or in any very violent emotions of the soul, our ideas may approach to our impres-

27

sions: As on the other hand it sometimes happens, that our impressions are so faint and low, that we cannot distinguish them from our ideas."[2] The fancies of liars may acquire by repetition the force and vivacity of realities: memories may become so faint as to be "perfect ideas"; and in fever and madness ideas may be no less forceful than impressions, as in a coma perceptions may be indistinguishable in force and vivacity. In thus failing to stand as an analysis of the species of perception, Hume's analysis of the perceptions of the mind fails to establish the doctrine that every genuine simple idea is the copy of a simple impression. Were Malebranche challenged to point out the prototype of his idea of necessary connection, he might reply that his present idea was as compelling in its vivacity as any sense-perception he could recall, and as such not distinguishable from a perception of the senses.

The proposition that every image is a copy might be true, and it still not follow that every idea is an image. Moreover, as Mr. Laird has remarked, though all ideas were images, it would be a wise idea that knew its own impression. Hume in effect argues that all images being by his definition ideas, all ideas therefore are images. And to complete his principle, he assumes that in being copies, ideas know their originals.

Having exhibited the species into which perception may be analysed, Hume describes the principles of synthesis in virtue of which there exist the complex ideas of relations, modes, and substances.[13] Since the imagination can effect a separation wherever a difference appears, and can compound the ideas thus separated into fancies, the operations of imagination would be wholly unpredictable, "were it not guided by some universal principles, which render it, in some measure, uniform with itself in all times and places."[10] Hume thus agrees with those who find a mere separateness of ideas incompatible with an intelligible description of experience, and proceeds to explain why it is that in all experience not that of mere fancy, ideas uniformly appear not in isolation, but in association.

Imagination as fancy Hume has described as the "principle" of separation and transposition of ideas. Imagination is now considered as it is uniformly guided in "the union and cohesion" of its images. Fancies, or "perfect" ideas, are separate and more or less free from routine associations. The operations of imagination are not alone fugacious, however; for we find in experience that they are also uniform and coherent. In no case of the union and cohesion of distinct images is the connection to be regarded as an inseparable one; "for that has been already excluded from the imagination."[10] An "inseparable connection" would be a "real" connection; one whose contradictory were inconceivable. Since whatever is distinct is separable, the distinct elements of a complex image will be united only by the force of association; a force of attraction which Hume in effect compares to the attraction of gravitation.

As "qualities" of this gentle force, Hume enumerates resemblance, contiguity, and cause and effect. His innovation here is the inclusion of cause and effect among the laws of association. Since he is later on to examine this relation "to the bottom," Hume will at this juncture say no more about it.[11] Yet the fact that here, at the outset of the *Treatise*, the relation of cause and effect is regarded as a law of association, is no more than consistent with Hume's final conclusion as to the nature of that relation.

It is "plain," Hume thinks, that resembling ideas will be associated together. It is evident also that perceptions contiguous in time or place will be found associated in recollection. And the force of association which will unite two "objects" "when the one is immediately resembling, contiguous to, or the cause of the other," will unite them also when their relation is mediated by a third object.[11] Since the "full extent" of the powers of association by resemblance, contiguity, cause and effect, is limited only by the fact that as the mediation increases in complexity the force of the association weakens, this mediation "may be carried on to a great length."[11] To such a length, indeed, that it is in ideas united in their complexity by association that the fundamental metaphysical categories of relation, mode, and substance are to be found.[13]

The dogma that what is distinguishable is separable plainly begs the question of a logical connection between ideas. Since the dogma applies also to impressions, Hume's famous question of the logical necessity of the causal relation is, it may be insisted, begged before it is raised. Yet, though the imagination can produce a separation wherever there is a distinction, the fancies which result are ideas cut off from the associated images constituting the imagination which is "in some measure uniform with itself in all times and places." Fancies are ideas (whether simple or complex) existing in separation from the normal course of imagery, within which distinct images exist not in isolation, but in complexes of which the force of association is the principle of union.[12]

Mr. Laird points out that Hume speaks frequently of association as a relation. This is indefensible, in Mr. Laird's opinion, because "perceptions must *be* similar in order to be associated *by* similarity, and . . . they must *have been* contiguous in order to be associated *by* contiguity."*

This criticism raises the question of the nature of relations in Hume's view; a question to which we now turn.

The word relation, Hume finds, is used in two different senses. It means either "that quality, by which two ideas are connected together in the imagination . . . after the manner above explained," or it refers to "that particular circumstance, in which, even upon the arbitrary union of two ideas in the fancy we may think proper to compare them." It is then either a relation of association or a relation of comparison to which we refer when we use the word. Since, moreover, the first sense is always that of "common language," Hume takes it that a relation of association is what is meant by the established meaning of the term, it being "only in philosophy, that we extend it to mean any particular subject of comparison, without a connecting principle."[13, 14] The three qualities connecting ideas in imagination Hume calls natural relations. That they are characterized as natural is perhaps because they are natural to the mind in the sense that without them the customs which constitute the understanding could not exist.† The pervasiveness of association is

* J. Laird, *Hume's Philosophy of Human Nature*, p. 42.

† Compare the "liaisons naturelles" in Malebranche's theory of the imagination. ". . . elles sont semblables généralement dans tous les hommes; elles sont absolument nécessaires à la conservation de la vie." *Recherche de la Vérité*, Edn. Bouillier, Vol. I, p. 152.

such that "its effects are everywhere conspicuous." But its causes "are mostly unknown, and must be resolved into *original* qualities of human nature, which I pretend not to explain."[13] An original constituent of human nature, the force of association is not derivative, and therefore not to be explained by a search for its origins.

Resemblance, contiguity, and cause and effect are the names both of natural and philosophical relations. For by a diligent consideration of the matter, Hume finds seven ways in which perceptions may be compared. Of these the most extensive is resemblance; for wherever no resemblance appears there no comparison can be made.

Second in importance is identity, or the persistence of things through time. After resemblance, this relation is the most universal. For all "beings" of any duration may be compared in that respect. And following substantial identity in universality are the relations of space and time, "which are sources of an infinite number of comparisons, such as *distant*, *contiguous*, *above*, *below*, *before*, *after*, etc." And quantity and number are "another very fertile source" of comparisons.

Degrees of quality "form a fifth species of relation." Hues differing only in depth may be compared in point of saturation. The sixth species of relation is contrariety, of which the ideas of existence and non-existence are the only example. For they alone of all ideas are contrary. Yet, as we shall see, Hume denies that we have an idea of existence. And from what an idea of non-existence could be copied, it is not easy to see.

Cause and effect is the seventh philosophical relation, "as well as a natural one." The resemblance "implied in this relation," Hume will explain later on.[14, 15]

Throughout this section philosophical relations are so designated as to suggest that these relations of comparison are qualifying predicates or real connections distinguishable from the "objects" compared. For philosophical relations are referred to as "qualities," "species," and "kinds." These references would seem to suggest, at the least, that universals as species or classes of which the objects compared are individuals or members, are regarded by Hume as real, not nominal.

Yet Hume wants us to understand that such is not his meaning. To the word "resemblance" as it is first used in the course of his exposition of his theory of abstract ideas, Hume appends the following lengthy and important footnote. "It is evident, that even different simple ideas may have a similarity or resemblance to each other; nor is it necessary that the point or circumstance of resemblance should be distinct or separable from that in which they differ. *Blue* and *green* are different simple ideas, but are more resembling than *blue* and *scarlet*; though their perfect simplicity excludes all possibility of separation or distinction. It is the same case with particular sounds, and tastes and smells. These admit of infinite resemblances upon the general appearance and comparison, without having any common circumstance the same. And of this we may be certain, even from the very abstract terms *simple idea*. They comprehend all simple ideas under them. These resemble each other in their simplicity. And yet from their very nature, which excludes all composition, this circumstance, in which they resemble, is not distinguishable nor separable from the rest. It is the same with all the degrees in any quality. They are all resembling, and yet the quality, in any individual, is not distinct from the degree."[637] Like simplicity, resemblance is an abstract term. In no case of simple ideas (or impressions) compared, is there to be discriminated "any common circumstance" of which "resemblance" is the name. This must be so, Hume argues, because the ideas are simple, and hence such that within them there can be nothing over and above what they themselves intrinsically are. Thus, given two simple ideas (or impressions), p_1 and p_2, to say that p_1 and p_2 are resembling or the same, is not to say anything *about* p_1 and p_2; it is to say nothing *more* than that p_1 is p_1 and p_2 is p_2. Resemblance, or sameness, then, are not proper names of characters or qualities over and above the simple ideas compared. The statement "p_1 and p_2 are similar" means what is meant by the statement "p_1 and p_2 are comparable"; and this statement means what is meant by "p_1 is p_1 and p_2 is p_2."

Resemblance, then, is not the proper name of a qualifying predicate or of a connection of any sort. In Hume's view, resemblance is reduced to the qualitative identity of simple ideas. They are comparable not in virtue of any quality distinct from themselves, which might be called "their resemblance," but in virtue of their intrinsic natures alone. Likewise, two complex ideas, $M N O P_1$ and $P_2 Q R S T$, will be comparable in point of constituent P, itself qualitatively identical in P_1 and P_2. Hume is thus assuming that resemblance may mean what is meant by qualitative identity. And he is assuming that a single qualitative identity P may be numerically distributed in P_1 and P_2.

It is also the case, he asserts, that "the quality, in any individual, is not distinct from the degree." It is thus maintained that the degree of saturation of a hue (say) is intrinsic to the hue, and hence not distinguishable from it. Again, blue and green are more resembling than blue and scarlet.[637] But the degree of resemblance here is not distinguishable from the several qualities themselves, as is proved by "their perfect simplicity." Hence in any case of a comparison of degrees, all that is involved is exhausted in the qualities compared.

Taken as relations of comparison, the remaining philosophical relations are to be understood in the same way. Thus substantial identity is, as Hume finds, not the proper name of anything (such as a substratum) distinguishable from the perceptual phenomena of which selves and perceived bodies consist. Likewise, cause and effect is found not to be the name of a necessary connection between perceptual events; and that the repetition of causes and effects is not a quality of the events repeated, Hume will fully explain. But he does not definitely attempt, it would seem, to make out the sense in which quantity and number are no more than philosophical relations. And the difficulties peculiar to his theories of space and time must be reserved for separate treatment.

The natural relation, being a "principle of union," is precisely what the philosophical relation is not; it is a real connection. Yet this does not imply that, in any case of the natural relation of resemblance, what is resembling is as such the connecting fact. For the principle of union is the attraction of association. Since the items associated are the impressions and ideas which, in their intrinsically resembling or qualitatively identical respects, *are* the philosophical relations they exhaustively constitute, the natural relation of resemblance differs from the philosophical one only in point of the attraction of association. The phrase, "natural relation of resemblance," refers to the natural origin and the connecting power of the relation, and also to the qualitative identity of the impressions and ideas associated. The naturalness and connecting power of association are inexplicable, as is also the fact of the association of resembling perceptions. What may be explained is merely that this resemblance is not a relation, or anything distinct from the respects in which perceptions are qualitatively identical. In any case of its existence, then, the natural relation of resemblance will be a case of that philosophical relation operated on by the gentle force of association.

Hume's theory of natural relations is thus a combination of his view of association as a natural fact with his theory of philosophical relations. No philosophical relation or relation of comparison is a connecting principle. The resemblance by which ideas are associated is not distinguishable from the ideas themselves. Any case of association by resemblance will then be exhausted in the intrinsically similar ideas *and* the attraction of association. Likewise, contiguity as such being exhausted in any case of intrinsically contiguous ideas or impressions, the nature of associations by contiguity will always be exhausted in the intrinsically contiguous content and the force of association. The *philosophical relation* of cause and effect, we shall see, *is* exhausted in the succession and contiguity of sense-perceptions. Such perceptions are the content of the habits formed by their association thus to constitute the natural relation of cause and effect.

Had Hume used resemblance and contiguity as the names of real connections, it would be true on his view that association presupposes relation in that sense; and his use of relation and association as equivalent terms would be indefensible. Since, however, for him resemblance and contiguity as such are abstract terms, whose meaning is wholly exhausted in any given case of intrinsically similar ideas or intrinsically contiguous impressions, there is no assumption of resemblance and contiguity as connections. The sole principle of connection is association. Hence association does not presuppose, but *is* relation in the single sense in which, for Hume, "to relate" is "to connect."[10]

II

Something of the significance of Hume's view of resemblance appears when it is noticed that Nominalism, as a theory admitting of several variants, might be described as consisting in part in the contention that the predication of resemblance involves no reference to a quality or character distinct from and common to the entities compared. The Nominalist, if he is to do more than merely occupy his position, must explain the nature and function of abstract adjectives and class names. Such terms cannot, in his view, refer to a common character or form. Yet, in fact, they are employed in all discourse, and employed with significance. Hence Hume's theory of philosophical relations invites the question, to what do abstract adjectives and class names refer? His answer to this question is his theory of abstract ideas.

After praising Berkeley's discovery about the nature of abstract ideas, Hume proceeds to confirm the conclusion of that philosopher with some arguments which he hopes will establish it conclusively. Accordingly, he first advances an argument which he apparently takes to be the accepted proof of the doctrine combated by Berkeley.[18] Abstract terms must either (1) represent all possible particular degrees of quantity and quality, *or* (2) represent no particular degree of quantity and quality. But abstract terms can represent all possible degrees of quantity and quality only if the capacity of the mind is infinite, which is absurd. Therefore, the second alternative, that abstract terms represent no particular degree of quantity and quality, must be true.[17, 18]

Hume denies that this proposition is true by an alleged and elaborate proof of its contradictory. He then proceeds to establish the first alternative, but so modified as no longer to imply the absurdity that finite minds are infinite in capacity.

That abstract ideas "represent no particular degree either of quantity or quality," Hume denies on the familiar ground, "that it is utterly impossible to conceive any quantity or quality without forming a precise notion of its degree."[18] That such is the case, Hume seeks to maintain by three lines of argument. The first of these is that in no case is either quantity or quality distinguishable from any concrete quantity or quality. For "it is evident at first sight, that the precise length of a line is not different or distinguishable from the line itself; nor the precise degree of any quality from the quality."[18, 19] Since we can separate only what we can distinguish, and since no abstract qualities and quantities can be distinguished within concrete experience, there can be no abstract ideas.

Hume next argues that "no impression can become present to the mind, without being determined in its degrees both of quantity and quality,"[19] and that ideas are copies of these determinate impressions: therefore an abstract idea is "a contradiction in terms."[19] In his third argument here, Hume hardly improves on his second. It is a principle "generally received in philosophy" that every existent is an individual. Hence in fact there can be no abstractions. What is impossible "in fact and reality" must be also impossible "in idea." We must then conclude that "abstract ideas are . . . in themselves individual, however they may become general in their representation."[20]

The alleged "principle" that every existent is an individual plainly begs the question of abstract ideas. Hume's second argument, assuming as it does that to be an idea is to be an image, also begs the question. So also does his first. For it rests on a definition of experience as consisting of impressions and ideas, and therefore excludes abstract ideas by definition.

Hume now proceeds to advance his own theory of the matter; a theory on which the first alternative that abstract ideas represent all degrees of a quality or quantity is established. Since this has been "esteemed absurd" by philosophers, it will be Hume's aim to show

"That though the capacity of the mind be not infinite, yet we can at once form a notion of all possible degrees of quantity and quality, in such a manner at least, as, however imperfect, may serve all the purposes of reflection and conversation."[18] Although, in so doing, he takes his departure from the Berkeleian doctrine that abstract ideas are particular ones which have "become general in their representation," Hume develops that doctrine into a theory which would appear to be his own.

The five main points of this theory may be stated as follows.

The repeated experience of resembling perceptions engenders a habit in the imagination. In virtue of this habit, the occurrence of a similar perception tends to evoke complex ideas of those past.

When we find perceptions to be similar in certain respects, we apply to them the same name; despite apparent differences in other respects.

As a result of the repeated use of the same name for perceptions that are in certain respects qualitatively similar, there develops another association; this time between the abstract term or name thus used and the habit in imagination wherein images of perceptions thus named are associated.

"After we have acquired a custom of this kind,

43

the hearing of that name revives the idea of one of these objects, and makes the imagination conceive it with all its particular circumstances and proportions."[20] It is thus as a result of this second association or habit that the hearing of the name alone suffices to incite the primary habit to produce an image of certain qualities of the present perception.

The word in question will have been often applied to other perceptions, differing in many respects from the idea thus evoked. And "the word not being able to revive the idea of all these individuals, only touches the soul, if I may be allowed so to speak, and revives that custom, which we have acquired by surveying them."[20] When both the primary habit and that of the association between the primary habit and the name are not "entirely perfect," "the mind may not be content with forming the idea of only one individual, but may run over several, in order to make itself comprehend its own meaning, and the compass of that collection, which it intends to express by the general term."[22] But in the measure that these two habits become "entire" or "perfect," the hearing of the name results neither in the recollection of all of the images associated in the primary habit, nor even in a large number of them. The result is either that one alone is evoked, together with a "readiness" or "power" of the imagination, to supply others, *or* in no more than the readiness or power.

Thus would Hume show to be groundless the alleged necessity that the idea of man should represent "men of all sizes and all qualities."[18] The associated images constituting the concretion in imagination with which the term man is associated "are not really and in fact present to the mind, but only in power. . . ."[20] In using the abstract term "man" we do not "draw them [the images associated] all out distinctly in the imagination, but keep ourselves in a readiness to survey any of them, as we may be prompted by a present design or necessity."[20]

Lest the term "readiness" here seem a weak substitute for an unequivocal statement on a crucial issue, it may be well to point out that in the next sentence, Hume goes on to say what he means by this "readiness" or "power" of the imagination. The hearing of any word or sentence "raises up" not only a single idea or complex of ideas, as the case may be, but also "a certain custom"; viz. that with which the word is associated. This custom, when "prompted by a present design or necessity," will "produce"[21] any other idea "for which we may have occasion."[21] Since association as such is a "force," habits of association may with some propriety be called "powers." The "readiness" of the

45

imagination, to which Hume here refers, is thus the liveliness of those customs with which names are associated.

An abstract idea, then, is a particular idea or complex of ideas associated by usage[22] with a name, which, by that same usage, is associated with the custom, or concretion of imagery, to which the particular image present belongs. In the constitution of an abstract idea there thus is (*a*) the particular image or set of images, (*b*) the name or descriptive phrase, (*c*) the association by usage of the name with the particular image, and (*d*) the further association of both the name and the particular image with the custom or concretion of imagery from which the image is derived. There are, then, in the constitution of an abstract idea two systems of association; that of the resembling imagery, and that of the name with this first system. To say of an abstract idea that it is at once particular in existence and general in significance then means that the idea evoked by the term or sentence heard is particular; while, at the same time, the concretion of imagery whence this idea is evoked, and with which the name also is associated, is by that same association also "raised up," and, in its capacity to furnish more ideas resembling the presented idea, constitutes the general reference of that particular idea.

The truth of his theory of abstract ideas, "so contrary to that, which has hitherto prevailed in philosophy,"[24] Hume regards as certain.* The only difficulty in the matter that can remain, he thinks, is that of the nature of the custom which is the general representation of abstract names. "To explain the ultimate causes of our mental actions is impossible."[22] "The most proper method, in my opinion, of giving a satisfactory explication of this act of the mind is by producing other instances which are analogous to it. . . ."[22] Proceeding by "experience and analogy," Hume goes on to find relevant cases of the existence and operation of custom. We have ordinarily no adequate idea of any great number, such as "a thousand," which may be mentioned. We possess only the power of producing such an idea in virtue of our habit of calculating in decimals. Again, there are cases of habits whose operation is provoked by the hearing of one word, such as verses learned by

* ". . . 'tis certain *that* we form the idea of individuals, whenever we use any general term; *that* we seldom or never can exhaust these individuals; and *that* those, which remain, are only represented by means of that habit, by which we recall them, whenever any present occasion requires it. This then is the nature of our abstract ideas and general terms; and 'tis after this manner we account for the foregoing paradox, *that some ideas are particular in their nature, but general in their representation.* A particular idea becomes general by being annex'd to a general term; that is, to a term, which from a customary conjunction has a relation to many other particular ideas, and readily recalls them in the imagination."[22]

rote. And, finally, when we use such terms as government, church, negotiation, conquest, ordinarily we do not have in mind the information requisite for adequate definitions of these terms. Yet despite this "imperfection, we may avoid talking nonsense on these subjects."[23]

In this connection we may notice with Hume a truly "extraordinary circumstance."[21] The mind, in so far as it is any one of these habits, once aroused by the perception of an abstract name, is then in readiness to prevent errors in our use of the name. "Thus should we mention the word triangle, and form the idea of a particular equilateral one to correspond to it, and should we afterward assert *that the three angles of a triangle are equal to each other*, the other individuals of a scalenum and isosceles, which we overlooked at first, immediately crowd in upon us, and make us perceive the falsehood of this proposition, though it be true with relation to that idea, which we had formed."[21] More generally still, Hume's point here may be illustrated in this way. Let $a_1, a_2 \ldots a_n$ be images with which P is associated. Suppose, then, that in making statements in which P occurs we have in mind a_1, which will of course differ in some respects from the members of the range $a_2 \ldots a_n$. Should our statements about a_1 refer to some respect in which it differs from the members of $a_2 \ldots a_n$, and hence to a respect to which P does not habitually refer, the habit, with which P is associated, will at once produce enough of the members of the range to make it at once plain that P is being misused; that is to say, used in a way that is incompatible with the habitual usage of that name. This, in Hume's language, is why the definition of a term involves the rules of its use in propositions.

When the customs are not very "perfect," the resulting misuse of abstract terms will cause a tangle among the contents of the customs themselves, thus giving rise to confused inferences and sophistry. But this occurs mainly when ideas are "abstruse" and "compounded," so that their association with their technical terms is not firmly established. When the custom is "more entire," as is normally the case in the usage of a native language, we seldom make such mistakes. "Nay, so entire is the custom," Hume says, "that the very same idea . . . may be employed in different reasonings, without any danger of mistake."[21] In the case of such customs as constitute the image-content of a language native to its user, the same image may be associated with different abstract terms, and hence with different rules of use. The image of a particular square may thus serve us both in our inferences about squares and about figures.

Hume thus points out the further "circumstance" in his theory of abstract ideas, that in virtue of its association with different names, the same *image* may function differently as a symbol.

It would appear to be plain that Hume's theory of abstract ideas is not merely a theory about names. In Hume's view, the habit of imagination to which an abstract term refers, consists of a more or less elaborate concretion of images united not as a result of relations logical in any sense, but of the natural relations of association. Hence the abstract term, in referring to (in virtue of its association with) the habit, refers to a wholly concrete thing. The conclusion that Hume's "scepticism with regard to the senses" reduces body to a name is therefore mistaken. For, to anticipate by way of illustration, the *referent* of the general name "body" will be all those habits in imagination which are associated with such names as "house," "store," etc. These various habits are at one in consisting of the images of such impressions and their associated ideas as appear with the constancy and coherence which are for Hume the mark of perceived bodies. The *reference* of our belief in matter will consist of the associations of these habits with their names: while the *referent* of that belief, far from being a mere name, will be those very habits themselves. They are the concrete and ready evidence of a repetition in experience of the constant and coherent perceptions which such habits, in their persistence, represent.

Nothing is more admirable, Hume thinks, than "the readiness with which the imagination suggests its ideas."[24] It is as if all ideas were present to a mind which had only to use them to its habitual purposes; whereas, in fact, there may be present only one idea and the felt readiness of its associated custom. The vivacity of this readiness in imagination, "though it be always most perfect in the greatest geniuses, and is properly what we call a genius, is however inexplicable by the utmost efforts of human understanding."[24] The genius of the understanding consists in neither impressions nor ideas, in neither memories nor fancies, but in the imagination that is the various concretions of imagery which are "the general representations" of abstract ideas.

The answer to be given to the questions, to what do abstract adjectives and class names refer, may now be plain. An abstract term in discourse will refer to, i.e. be associated with, that habit or concretion of images, any one of which will be in some respect or other what is ordinarily designated by that term in discourse. The reference itself is then the very habit in virtue of which that term in discourse is habitually used to refer to any one of a set of resembling images, or experiential content. The reference is thus always definite, and may so be felt. But in being thus definite, the reference is also general. It is general not because it refers to a resemblance as such, but rather because it refers to some respect or other of a particular image which, in that respect, is qualitatively identical with other images associated to form a habit. Since the reference is always to this or that particular idea or determinate respect, the reference is always definite. And since the reference is to *any* one of numerically different yet qualitatively identical content, in being thus definite the reference is also general.

The reference of an abstract term could refer to *all* the contents of a particular concretion, only if it were a reference to their resemblance as such; a reference, that is to say, to a distinguishable aspect of themselves, itself having an ontological status distinct from that of the contents themselves. The reference, however, is to no such abstract form; but rather to *any* one of numerically different and qualitatively identical contents of experience. Had Hume used "resemblance" to mean an idea or form in which image-contents must participate that they may be resembling, he would have used the term to

mean the abstract resemblance which his theory
denies, rather than the intrinsic qualitative
identity which his theory both of philosophical
relations and abstract ideas assumes to be the
proper meaning of "resemblance." Since, however,
it is not in the former but in the latter sense
that he uses the term, Hume's theory of association by resemblance is consistent with his denial
of abstract ideas.

The universals denied on this theory are those
of species or classes alone. It has been pointed
out* that Hume (like Berkeley) takes for granted
the repetition of impressions and ideas. In that
they are assumed to be repeatable irrespective
of space and time, the constituents of perceptions
are assumed to be universals in that restricted
sense. With regard to the repetition of selfsame
qualities, Hume may consult his own experience.
But his description of that experience is incompatible with the assumed recurrence of perceptions.
For perceptions are "perishing existences"; also,
they are "individuals," or "substances." Hence
both in existence and in nature perceptions are
unique, and therefore not repeatable.

The way is not open to the suggestion that
Hume might have distinguished between the
essence or character of a perception and its
existence or occurrence. For in his view the

* A. N. Whitehead, *Process and Reality*, p. 186.

existence of a perception is one with its character. "The idea of existence, then, is the very same with the idea of what we conceive to be existent. To reflect on anything simply, and to reflect on it as existent, are nothing different from each other. That idea, when conjoined with the idea of any object, makes no addition to it."[66, 67] Hence existence is not a qualifying predicate. There is no distinguishable quality in virtue of which a hundred possible dollars differ from a hundred actual dollars.

In support of this contention, Hume advances the following argument. Every perception is "conceived as existent." On this fact a dilemma may be based; "the idea of existence must either be derived from a distinct impression, conjoined with every perception or object of our thought, or must be the very same with the idea of the perception or object." Since there is no distinct impression of existence, the idea of existence is simply any and every existing idea.

The force of this dilemma is vitiated by the falsity of the dogma that an idea must be the copy of an impression. Yet, on the view that existence is not a qualifying predicate, existence can in no case be distinguished from essence. The repetition of perceptions is a fact for which Hume does not, and, it would seem, cannot account; and which he must, nevertheless, assume.

III

The question whether space and time, as analysed by Hume, can in any sense be philosophical relations, may now be considered. If there is a sense in which space and time as so analysed are neither philosophical nor natural relations, then it will be plain that Hume's theory of relations is inadequate to space and time as relational.

Hume's "system concerning space and time consists of two parts, which are intimately connected together."[39] The first of these consists of arguments alleged to demonstrate that space and time cannot be infinitely divisible, the second of a positive theory of space and time as being essentially sensuous in nature.

To consider these parts in order: Hume argues first of all that the capacities of the mind being finite, it is therefore plain that no idea can be infinitely divisible.[26-7] This being noticed, it is at once obvious that in the division of ideas "the imagination reaches a *minimum* . . . which cannot be diminished without a total annihilation."[27] What is true in this respect of ideas is found to be the case also with the impressions of the senses. In order to understand that the maximum of divisibility is the minimum of perceivability, we have only to withdraw from a spot of ink until we just lose sight of it; for this makes it "plain, that the moment before it vanished the image or impression was perfectly indivisible."[27] Thus the minimum area perceptible is simply asserted to be the limit of division.

Hume now goes on to assert that "the relations, contradictions and agreements" of ideas which are adequate to their objects must likewise apply to those objects themselves. Since a finite mind can divide no idea *ad infinitum*, extension itself must therefore consist of finite parts. Furthermore, our ideas necessarily being finite, and what they copy therefore being finite also, the assertion that extension is infinitely divisible is the plain absurdity that what is finite contains an infinite number of parts.

The last one of the grounds on which Hume rejects the conception of extension as infinitely divisible is a "very strong and beautiful" argument for which he has the authority of de Malezieu.[30 n. 2] Since extension as infinitely divisible "is always a number, according to the common sentiment of metaphysicians, and never resolves itself into any unit or indivisible quantity"; and since existence applies primarily to units, it follows that extension as infinitely divisible "can never at all exist."[30]

These arguments against the infinite divisibility of space hold equally against that of time. In this latter connection, however, there is a

further argument, in itself sufficient to demonstrate that time is not infinitely divisible. The
"property" of time which "in a manner constitutes
its essence" is the succession of its parts. This
being so, to assert time to be infinitely divisible
would be "an arrant contradiction."[31] For if the
parts of time were divisible *ad infinitum*, there
could be no succession, but only an infinite
number of co-existent moments of time.

Hume now turns to the constructive part of
his system, which is to give the correct account
of the idea of extension. This idea, he says, is
acquired by our "considering the distance between" visible bodies. What, then, is the character
of the perceptions thus considered? That they
will be perceptions of the senses is plain, since
they can hardly be passions, emotions, desires,
or aversions. "But my senses convey to me only
the impressions of coloured points, disposed in
a certain manner."[34] We must then conclude the
idea of extension to be a copy of these points
"and of the manner of their appearance."[34]

The nature of the abstract idea of extension,
as opposed to this or that copy, is no less easy to
explain. As a result of our experience of points
of various hues in this "certain disposition"
characteristic of extension, "we omit the peculi-
arities of colour, as far as possible, and found
an abstract idea merely on that disposition of

points, or manner of appearance, in which they agree."[34] So important to his argument here is this "order" or "disposition" of coloured points that Hume sees in it a resemblance by which "the impressions of touch are found to be similar to those of sight in the disposition of their parts."[34] Thus, in accordance with Hume's theory of abstract ideas, any "copy" of coloured or sensible points, ordered as is characteristic of extension, may be the particular content of the abstract idea in question.

Turning now to the idea of time, Hume finds it to be derived from "some perceivable succession of changeable objects." Since these "objects" may be ideas as well as impressions, which in turn may be not only of sensation but also of reflection, the idea of time is an abstract idea whose concrete referent is of "a still greater variety than that of space, and yet is represented in the fancy by some particular individual idea of a determinate quantity and quality."[35] That the succession which "in a manner constitutes the essence"[31] of time must be perceived, is Hume's main point here.[35] For the fact that the parts of time are not co-existent but successive is what distinguishes time from space. Hence, were this succession such as to be unperceived (as in the example adduced by Mr. Locke of the burning coal made to describe a full circle when rapidly wheeled around) there would be only contiguous impressions to be copied, from which no idea of time could be derived. But this perception of succession is not, Hume insists, the awareness of anything distinct from the perceptions themselves in their "manner" as successive. "The idea of time is not derived from a particular impression mixed up with others, and plainly distinguishable from them; but arises altogether from the manner, in which impressions appear to the mind, without making one of the number."[36] This "manner" is the succession of perceptions; and the awareness of it is the perception of succession.

That Hume's opinions in the matters of space and time are unsatisfactory has often been explained. The argument that, because the capacities of the mind are finite, we cannot frame infinite ideas, assumes that there is no difference between an idea of infinity and an infinite idea; an assumption which is of course a consequence of Hume's doctrine of impressions and ideas. Again, his arguments against infinite divisibility simply assume that the parts in question can be only aliquot or constituent parts; and in a footnote[30] he dismisses as "frivolous" the objection that such is not the case. In his references to "bodies *vastly* more minute than those which appear to the senses"[48] and to "the smallest atom of the animal spirits of an insect a thousand times less than a mite,"[28] Hume grants us ideas which cannot be images, but are the results of "sound reason,"[48] thus contradicting his "first principle."

It has been pointed out that Hume takes no steps to explain the dispositions and the manner which are for him characteristic of space and time. In view of his theory of relations as philosophical, this neglect might seem to be not an omission, but rather the implicit assumption of the adequacy of that theory of relations to the explanation of spatial and temporal orders. This would mean that since no philosophical relation, or relation of comparison, is a connection of any sort, space and time, regarded philosophically, are not kinds of connection. It is then no less than consistent with this view of relations that the dispositions and manners in question are not dealt with as though they were distinguishable qualities or connections. For as resemblance in this view is intrinsic to perceptions that are comparable, just so the manner that is succession, and the disposition that is spatial order are respectively assumed to be intrinsic to successive perceptions and to those perceptions properly called spatial. That Hume asserts a distance to consist of contiguous coloured points, but does not attempt to explain the meaning here of "disposition," would then suggest that over and above coloured points thus intrinsically ordered there can be nothing to explain; but only the intrinsically ordered points themselves.

This would mean that in Hume's view actual spaces are qualitative; that they are in no respect distinct from the qualitative character of the intrinsically ordered coloured points. Thus, as Mr. Laing has said, the distance between the outspread fingers of a hand is an impression; and one which cannot be had apart from the perception of the outspread fingers. Similarly, the contiguity of the fingers of a clenched fist is an impression which contributes to constitute the perception of the fist.

That spaces and times are qualitative would indeed appear to be Hume's view of the matter. And it would be open to him to deal with distance, contiguity, etc., *as such* as he does deal with resemblance and degrees of quality. When we compare two distances, we compare them not in point of an abstract form in which they participate, but in point of the actual distances which they themselves are. Distance *as such*, then, is intrinsic to actual distances: it may be regarded as a philosophical relation, in every case exhausted in actual distances as compared. But, for a reason which Hume indicates, that distance *as such* may be a philosophical relation and intrinsic to actual

61

distances, cannot mean that any actual distance, *such as* that of 20 feet, is a philosophical relation and intrinsic to the impressions which that distance relates, as an identity in quality is intrinsic to its qualitative instances.

In his first list of relations as being among "the elements of this philosophy,"[13] Hume appears to regard all relations as being either philosophical or natural relations. Again, in his second list of relations,[69] space and time are classed with those relations which do not "depend entirely" on their ideas, but may be altered without any change in the ideas compared. Any case of resemblance will depend entirely on the ideas compared, because any alteration of the character of those ideas will be an alteration of the qualitative identity that is the resemblance. Likewise, distance *as such* will depend entirely on the ideas compared; for when the character of the compared distances is altered, what "distance as such" then refers to is altered. In a comparison of two distances there will be involved no more than the two distances Q and Q', and the philosophical relation of distance as such, of whose meaning as an abstract idea Q and Q' are in this case the exhaustive referent. But when it is said that A is at a distance Q from B, there is then no comparison. The actual distance may not be dealt with as may be the philosophical relation distance as such; for the distance Q is not a relation of comparison.

This would be true likewise of contiguity, above, below, before, and after, etc. Taken *as such* they may be regarded as being philosophical relations. But in finding that A is contiguous to B, that A is before B, etc., these relations are taken not as such, but rather such as may be the individual case. Thus, if the dispositions as such of the coloured points may be relations of comparison, the points as ordered constitute relations which can be neither philosophical nor natural. For though Hume finds contiguity to be a natural relation, he does not appear so to regard the other orders in space and time which he mentions. As relations neither of comparison nor of association, spaces and times are an anomaly in Hume's theory of relations; but an anomaly to which his theory of abstract ideas is adequate. The referent of "distance as such" would be a concretion in imagination of ideas of actual distances; ideas which would be associated because, as ideas of distances, they are the same. As we have no copy of resemblance *as such*, so we have no idea of abstract distance. But just as any idea will exhibit the intrinsic qualitative identity referred to by abstract resemblance, so any copy of a distance will be an instance of the referent of distance as such. And,

63

as "colour" is the name of any hue evoked in idea, so also an idea of a distance of 20 feet, say, in virtue of its qualitative identity with all other ideas of that distance, will "stand for" any number of them, as they form the concretion in imagination that is what is thus referred to by this particular idea of the distance of 20 feet.

CHAPTER II

The Critical Analysis of Causation and Substance

I

MODES and substances are among the subjects considered in Part I as being among the elements of Hume's philosophy. It has seemed best, however, to reserve that subject for separate treatment and, in view of the fact that Hume's theories in this connection are negative or critical as well as constructive in nature, to deal with his critical arguments apart from and before going on to his theories about our belief in substance. For the same reason his critique of causation will be considered apart from the full theory of causal inference to which it gives rise. In this way we may be better able to make out what is critical and what constructive in Hume's views of causation and substance.

It is sometimes said that Hume's analysis of causation and substance is so thoroughly dependent on his theory of ideas as to be quite vitiated by the falsity of that theory. With regard to each one of his major arguments as it is encountered, it may then be well to ask whether or not it depends on the false doctrine in question. And to the copy theory of ideas may be added another principle that Hume often employs, viz. that what is distinguishable is separable. For this is the principle of his atomism in psychology and logic.

Of the seven kinds of relation listed in Part I, four "depend entirely on the ideas which we compare together"; viz. resemblance, degrees in quality, contrariety, and proportion in quantity and number. Awareness of the first three of these is intuitive; the fourth being known ordinarily in inference. The sense in which these four relations "are the foundations of science" is a question to be discussed in a subsequent chapter. It is the case, however, that for Hume these four relations exhaust the content of intuitive and demonstrative knowledge; for no case of the three relations remaining is found to be either intuitively or demonstrably certain. Moreover, the greater part of Hume's *Treatise on the Human Understanding* is given not to the relations which afford know-ledge, but to those which are the content of belief.*

All reasoning is comparison, "and a discovery of those relations, either constant or inconstant, which two or more objects bear to each other."[73] This comparison may be made "either when both

---

* Part II is given to space and time; Sections 2 to 7 of Part IV and Section 6 of Part I deal with substance, and of Part III, Sections 2 to 16 deal with causation.

the objects are present to the senses, or when neither of them is present [and their copies are compared], or when only one" is present.[73] Resemblance, degrees in quality, and contrariety are thus directly perceived. Since in comparisons of substantial identity and time and place the mind is concerned only with what is actually there, these comparisons also are perceptions, not inferences. Cause and effect is the one relation by means of which a single impression present can be compared with a perception absent, but anticipated in imagination; "nor can the other two relations [i.e. substantial identity and time and place] be ever made use of in reasoning, except so far as they either affect or are affected by it."[74] The substantial identity of things present here and now may be compared in direct perception. But only on the assumption that the causes of a thing's existence remain unaltered may the continued existence of a thing beyond perception be inferred. Again, although times and places as such admit of comparison without inference, still any constancy or variation in such relations may be inferred to exist only as a result of causation. That relation, therefore, is the principle of all inferences about matters of fact.

Nothing exists which may not be considered as either a cause or an effect; "though it is plain there is no one quality, which universally belongs to all beings, and gives them title to that denomination."[75] Since, therefore, the origin of the idea of cause and effect is to be found in no quality of our perceptions, it must be derived from some relation between them. Hume at once finds two such relations: causes and effects are contiguous in space and time, and the cause is always prior in time to the effect.[75, 76]*

But contiguity and succession do not afford a complete idea of causation.[77] A thing at once contiguous and prior to another still might not be considered its cause. "There is a *necessary connection* to be taken into consideration, and that relation is of much greater importance than any of the other two above mentioned."[77] Necessary connection is then the defining characteristic of the causal relation. The impression from which this idea is derived is therefore the one we are looking for. Yet the only relations between impressions Hume has found so far are those of contiguity and succession, "which I have already regarded as imperfect and unsatisfactory."[77] And he proceeds to divide his problem into two

---

* In *Perception, Physics, and Reality*, pp. 120–2, Dr. Broad points out that Hume's proof of the temporal priority of causes is formally vicious. Hume himself seems to have had some doubts about its validity, for he writes: "If this argument appear satisfactory, 'tis well. If not, I beg the reader to allow me the same liberty, which I have used in the preceding case (i.e. that of contiguity), of supposing it such. For he shall find, that the affair is of no great importance."[76]

68

questions: why we believe that every event must have some cause or other; and why we believe that the same cause must *necessarily* produce the same effect.[78] Hume thus distinguishes the law of causality from the law of causation, and takes it that together they are what is meant by a necessary connection among events.

Though a "general maxim in philosophy," that every event must have a cause is not a matter of knowledge. This Hume demonstrates first on the grounds of his own view of the extent of knowledge. The law of causality may be identified neither with resemblance, degrees of quality, contrariety, nor proportions in quantity and number. The law is therefore not known to be true. Hume thinks that anyone who would controvert this conclusion will be obliged to exhibit a relation at once identical with causality and known by direct inspection, "which it will then be time enough to examine."[79]

He proceeds next to urge that the law in question is to be demonstrated by apagogic reasoning on no theory of knowledge, and therefore is "neither intuitively nor demonstrably certain."[79] That every event must have some cause or other means that the ideas of cause and effect are necessarily connected. Were this the case, it would be impossible that those ideas should be separable. Yet, since they are distinct, the ideas of cause and effect are separable; and the denial of their necessary connection involves no contradiction.[79, 80] Here Hume relies on the principle of his atomism. Yet he need not have done so; for the contradictory of the law of causality being not self-contradictory, that law is not demonstrable by apagogic reasoning.

Accordingly, all alleged demonstrations of the necessity of a cause are pronounced "fallacious and sophistical."[80] The arguments of Hobbes and Clarke are refuted on the way to an exposure of the *petitio* in Locke's version of the argument to the necessity of a cause from *nihil ex nihilo*. To deny that every event has some cause or other is to assert events either to be self-caused or to be caused by nothing. With respect to this alleged reduction to absurdity of the denial of causality, "It is sufficient only to observe, that when we exclude all causes we really do exclude them, and neither suppose nothing nor the object itself to be the causes of the existence; and consequently can draw no argument from the absurdity of these suppositions to prove the absurdity of that exclusion."[81] If it is true that everything must have some cause or other, then from the exclusion of all other causes it follows that events must be caused either by themselves or by nothing. But the truth of the law of causality being the point in question, to assert that the contradictory of the law implies things to be caused by nothing merely begs the question.[81, 82]

It is "still more frivolous" to argue to the necessity of a cause from the premise that cause and effect are correlative terms. That every husband must have a wife does not imply that in fact any man is married; and that every event properly called an effect must have a cause does not even tend to prove any event to be properly called an effect.[82]

It is to be noticed that Hume's examination of our alleged knowledge of the necessity for causes does not turn on his copy theory of ideas. The premise of his first argument is his own view of the scope of knowledge. The point of his second argument, that the contradictory of the law in question is conceivable, is made to depend on his dogma that what is distinguishable is separable. That dependence, we have noticed, is not necessary. And in his exposure of the *petitio* in both the argument to causality from *nihil ex nihilo*, and in that to the same conclusion from the fact that cause and effect are correlative terms, Hume depends on his insight alone.

The law of causality being neither intuitively nor demonstrably certain, whence the idea and the conviction with which it is held? It is plain that, "since it is not from knowledge or any scientific reasoning" that this idea is derived, it must "arise from observation and experience."[82] It is thus not by the way of any deduction from his copy theory of ideas, but rather because of the previously exposed incompetence of apagogic reasoning in the matter, that Hume turns to experience as the remaining alternative. The general question as to the origins of the idea in question in experience and observation Hume proposes to deal with by finding the answer to a more definite question; viz. what is the nature of our belief that the same cause must have the same effect.[82]

Since an inference can neither begin in nothing nor go on indefinitely, any causal inference will begin in "an immediate perception of our memory or senses."[83] Moreover, when the perception designated cause, or that designated effect, is alone preesnt, its correlative is inferred in idea. Causal inference thus contains a present perception, either of sense or memory, and an idea reached by inference. Hence there are three matters to be explained: "*First*, The original impression. *Secondly*, The transition to the idea of the connected cause or effect. *Thirdly*, The nature and qualities of that idea."[84] The causes of impressions of sensation are "perfectly inexplicable";[84] and as for the impressions of memory, we have already noticed that they can in practice be distinguished from fancies only in point of force and vivacity, and sometimes not at all.

Turning to the second question, *Of the inference from the impression to the idea*, Hume is first of all concerned to point out that this operation is not the discovery of an implication holding between impression and idea. Again relying on his dogma that what is distinguishable is separable, he roundly asserts: "There is no object, which implies the existence of any other if we consider these objects in themselves, and never look beyond the ideas we form of them. Such an inference would amount to knowledge, and would imply the absolute contradiction and impossibility of conceiving anything different."[86, 87] Since ideas, being distinct, are separable, in passing from the impression to its associated idea, that idea might be displaced and another substituted for it.

Here Hume bases his denial of a necessary connection between impressions and ideas on the dogma of his atomism, not on his copy theory of ideas. The conclusion to which Hume thus comes, however, would nevertheless appear to be sound with regard to individual things. For in virtue of the otherness of individuals, the existence of no individual thing may imply the existence of any other.* Moreover, Hume's full point here would also seem to be valid. For there is no contradiction

* Cf. R. E. Hobart, *Hume Without Scepticism*, *Mind*, N.S., Vol. 39.

in denying of any fact that it implies the existence of anything beyond itself. To this what is sometimes said to be the truth illustrated by Descartes' *Cogito ergo sum* may appear to be an exception. But that no state of consciousness can deny its own existence means that every state of consciousness will exist, not that *this* undeniable conscious state does or may imply the existence of anything beyond itself.

Since causal inference cannot be apagogic, it must be experiential in nature. And Hume proceeds to advance a general description of the experience that is causal inference. "The nature of experience is this. We remember to have had frequent instances of the existence of one species of objects; and also remember that the individuals of another species of objects have always attended them, and have existed in a regular order of contiguity and succession with regard to them." "We likewise call to mind their constant conjunction in all past instances. Without any farther ceremony, we call the one *cause* and the other *effect*, and infer the existence of the one from that of the other."[87] The full nature of the habit in association thus engendered Hume explains in the subsequent seven sections. Here, following Hume, the "new relation betwixt cause and effect" which we have "insensibly discovered" is to be considered.

Critical Analysis of Causation and Substance

The constant conjunction, which is our new relation, is the constant repetition of impressions and ideas conjoined in space and time. Neither "constancy" nor "repetition," however, are attributes of impressions and ideas constantly repeated. Hence our new-found relation is not the discovery of any distinguishable character of perceptions,* and therefore it "seems to advance us but very little on our way" in the search for necessary connection. Yet, though the discovery that we remember best those impressions and ideas whose repetition in contiguity and succession is constant does not tell us what necessary connection is, still it does indicate the origin of the inference from impression to idea. Turning now to examine the nature of that inference, Hume forecasts his conclusion: it may turn out that the connection depends on the inference, rather than that the inference depends on the connection.

So far, we have noticed that the transition from impression to idea derives somehow from the memory of experiences constantly conjoined. That being the origin of the inference, the question now is, "whether we are determined by reason to make the transition, or by a certain association and relation of perceptions."[88, 89] Hume has

---

* "For it implies no more than this, that like objects have always been placed in like relations of contiguity and succession; . . . we can never discover any new idea, and can only multiply, but not enlarge the objects of the mind."[88]

pointed out that the inference is not determined by the discovery of a connection the contradictory of which would be inconceivable. He now proceeds, and without reference either to his theory of ideas as copies, or to the principle of his atomism, to point out that the uniformity of nature is not demonstrable by apagogic reasoning, because its contradictory is conceivable.* "We can at least conceive a change in the course of nature; which sufficiently proves that such a change is not absolutely impossible."[89]

Nor, in default of certainty, may we have recourse here to probability. For since the relation of cause and effect is the principle of all inference about matters of fact, no inference to a probability can be independent of that relation. Hence probable reasoning will presume the future to resemble the past; evidently a presumption which cannot itself depend on probability.[90] The uniformity of nature being demonstrable neither by apagogic nor inductive reasoning, the question whether causal inference is the work of reason or imagination[88] is so far answered; and we return to the principles of union in the imagination as constituting the force of the inference from cause to effect.

* "Our foregoing method of reasoning will easily convince us, that there can be no *demonstrative* arguments to prove, *that those instances of which we have had no experience resemble those of which we have had experience.*"[89]

Hume takes his analysis thus far to have shown that our only notion of "cause and effect" is of "certain objects" constantly conjoined.[93] "We cannot penetrate into the reason of the conjunction. We only observe the thing itself, and always find that from the constant conjunction the objects acquire an union in the imagination."[93] Our notion of cause and effect, as so far disclosed, is no more than a philosophical relation. With regard to their constant repetition as contiguous and successive, causes and effects are comparable. Though both the "disposition" that is contiguity, and the "manner" that is succession be orders distinguishable from simple impressions and ideas thus disposed and mannered, "constancy" and "repetition" are in no sense qualifying predicates. Yet this must not obscure the fact that, in Hume's view, the constituents of the philosophical relation, viz. impressions and ideas intrinsically contiguous, successive and constantly conjoined, constitute the contents associated to form the natural relation of cause and effect. "Thus though causation be a *philosophical* relation, as implying contiguity, succession, and constant conjunction, yet it is only so far as it is a *natural* relation, and produces an union among our ideas, that we are able to reason upon it, or draw any inference from it."[94] And causation *is* more than a philosophical relation just "so far" as it *is* association.

The answer to our second question concerning the nature of the transition from impression to idea in causal inference is thus that the transition is the work of associations or habits in imagination, not of reason. So understood, the inference from impression to idea Hume declares to be "one part of the definition of an opinion or belief; that it is *an idea related to or associated with a present impression.*"[93] In the following six sections of Part III (viz. 7 to 14) the other parts of Hume's theory of belief are brought out and defended on the way to the conclusion that the idea of necessary connection derives from the felt force of the natural relation of cause and effect.

Hume's theory of causal inference will be considered in the next chapter. Here we shall proceed at once to Section 14, there "to return upon our footsteps" and ask about the idea of necessary connection. This means, as Hume at once reminds us, that we are looking for its origin, which he discovers to us at the top of the next page.[156] In sense experience there occur impressions that are intrinsically contiguous, successive, and constantly conjoined. Since a consideration of repeated impressions no more than repeats the same ideas, it would seem that we can go no further.

But at this point Hume abruptly announces that "upon further enquiry" he finds the consequences of repetition to be not always the same. "For after a frequent repetition, I find, that upon the appearance of one of the objects, the mind is *determined* by custom to consider its usual attendant, and to consider it in a stronger light upon account of its relation to the first object. It is this impression, then, or *determination*, which affords me the idea of necessity."[156] The original of the idea in question is thus found not in sense-experience, but in the internal impression of active habit.

Hume now proceeds to defend his conclusion against the opposing claims of Locke and the Cartesians. His defence opens with the assertion that the terms power, force, energy, necessity, connection, and productive quality, all being "nearly synonymous," no one may be used to define any other of them. Thus are rejected "all the vulgar definitions, which philosophers have given of power and efficacy."[157] The views of Locke, however, are given further consideration. According to that philosopher, we find changes in experience; and, inferring that somewhere there must be a power which could produce them, we thus arrive at the idea of power and efficacy. But "this explication is more popular than philosophical."[157] For reason alone (i.e. the comparison of ideas) can arrive at nothing new. And that every event requires a cause is not demonstrable.

Locke thus disposed of, Hume proceeds[158] to give a free translation from Malebranche of a summary of views on causation attributed to the scholastics.* Not only because these theories are "mixed and varied in a thousand different ways," but also because the notions of "substantial forms, and accidents, and faculties" all are unintelligible, we can find in such views nothing to our purpose. The general failure of philosophers to come to an understanding of power or necessity has at long last forced them to acknowledge the "ultimate force and efficacy of nature" to be unknown. Yet, though almost unanimous in this, philosophers are not at one in the inferences they draw from their agnosticism. As typical of the views of "some of them, the Cartesians in particular,"[159] Hume gives Malebranche's *a priori* proof that bodies are not causes, and a part of his main conclusion of which that proof is one premise. Since the definition of matter as extension excludes motion, in that definition nothing of the meaning of efficacy, or of the necessary communication of movement is to be found. From this reasoning the Cartesians conclude that God is the cause of the effects which matter, by definition, cannot produce.[159] But since we have no impression of the Deity from which this idea might be derived, the views of the Cartesians here are of no avail.

* *Recherche*, Edn. Bouillier, Vol. II, pp. 437, 438.

It must be concluded, Hume thinks, that whenever in the manner of the philosophers or the vulgar we speak of necessary connection or of power, we then have in mind "no distinct meaning, and make use only of common words. . . . But as it is more probable, that these expressions do here lose their true meaning by being *wrongly applied*, than that they never have any meaning, it will be proper to bestow another consideration on this subject . . .";[162] a consideration in the course of which Hume may make it plain that he does not mistake a repetition of impressions and ideas for an impression of repetition.

So far, he takes two points to have been established: (1) that along with constant conjunction the inference from cause to effect arises somehow; and (2) that the bare repetition of impressions and ideas can give rise to nothing new. But, since the idea of necessity does arise currently with this repetition, and yet is not duplicated in any one or any number of repeated impressions, "it follows that the repetition *alone* has not that effect, but must either *discover* or *produce* something new, which is the source of that idea."[163] That repetition can disclose nothing new is evident in the nature of the case. Furthermore, constant conjunction alone already has been shown to yield no connection or principle upon which inference might proceed. Constant repetition of conjoined perceptions is thus again found neither to discover nor to produce anything new.

But when to this repetition the gentle force of association is added, the case is altered. Hume now says that "the *observation* of the resemblance produces a new impression *in the mind*. . . ."[165] Yet how can the idea of necessity be, as Hume goes right on to say that it is, "the effect of this observation . . ."? Does that not suggest the assumption of a mental subject in whom a new impression is caused by repetition? Should the suggestion in question be pressed, and Hume's constructive theory of the self be thus ignored, a verbal victory would, perhaps, be easy. That being admitted, let us consider what Hume goes directly on to say. "The idea of necessity arises from some impression. There is no impression conveyed by our senses, which can give rise to that idea. It must, therefore, be derived from some internal impression, or impression of reflection. There is no internal impression, which has any relation to the present business, but that propensity, which custom produces, to pass from an object to the idea of its usual attendant. This therefore is the essence of necessity."[165] Thus Hume again affirms the idea of necessity to be derived, not from any impression of sensation, but from that impression of reflection which is the felt determination of those habits in imagination in which ideas of constantly repeated conjuncts come to be associated. The "observation" of which that idea is the effect is thus the felt awareness of those habits or customs. Although Hume has at such length explained that repetition or resemblance *alone* cannot yield the impression sought for, when he asserts the idea of necessity to be the effect of the observation of resemblance[165] he perhaps takes too much for granted in assuming that after the entire foregoing discussion the reader will take "resemblance" here to name not alone that philosophical relation, but also that natural relation of association. For it is the feeling[165] of the active habits of imagination which result from that natural relation in all cases of constant conjunction that is the internal impression, or the observation, of which the idea of power or necessity is an effect.

Mr. Whitehead finds it "difficult to understand why Hume exempts 'habit' from the same criticism as that applied to the notion of 'cause.' We have no 'impression' of 'habit,' just as we have no 'impression' of 'cause.' Cause, repetition, habit are all in the same boat."* Mr. Whitehead must mean that of necessary connection we have no impression of sensation, not that of it we have no impression at all; yet that such is his meaning is perhaps not plain. It would also be a mistake

* *Process and Reality*, p. 196.

to assert that in Hume's view there is no *internal* impression of habit. For in the feeling of the imagination as determined by custom there is the internal impression of habit.[156, 165]

That there is no impression of repetition is a point on which Hume insists at length. Repetition of impressions and ideas adds nothing to them, because "being repeated," like "being similar," is not a qualifying predicate. "But it is from this resemblance that the ideas of necessity, of power and of efficacy, are derived. These ideas, therefore, represent not anything, that does or can belong to the objects, that are constantly conjoined."[164] Here "resemblance" refers at once to the intrinsically similar objects constantly conjoined, and to the natural relation of association so named. Together these form the habit in imagination of which the felt determination is the impression of power or necessity. Copies of this impression will represent nothing of the objects as repeatedly similar; for their repetition and similarity as such are not qualifying predicates. Being copies of the felt determinations of habits, they will represent the felt power of the gentle force of association as that force, together with certain ideas, contributes to constitute a particular habit of imagination. "Cause," "habit," and "repetition" are not "in the same boat." For of the habits which are the natural relation of cause and effect we do

84

have impressions of reflection; whereas of repetition we can and need have on Hume's theory no impression at all. After the repeated and insistent consideration[163, 164, 165] which Hume gives the point that no repetition of impressions can be or yield an impression of repetition, the claim that he fails to see that very point is astonishing.

It is sometimes said that Hume reduces the relation of cause and effect to succession. The ground for this interpretation appears to be that the philosophical relation of cause and effect is exhausted in perceptions that are contiguous, successive, and constantly conjoined. Did Hume confine his conception of causation to his view of cause and effect as a philosophical relation, it might be concluded that he considers causation to be no more than uniform succession; and that, in his insistence on its uniformity, he had fallen into thinking of a repetition of impressions as being an impression of repetition. Since Hume's full view, as stated by himself,[94, 170] is that cause and effect is at once a philosophical *and* a natural relation, or habit in imagination of which there is an impression of reflection,[156, 165] this further insistence on the point may be excused only because by tendentious critics it is sometimes denied or passed over altogether.

Hume is aware of the paradoxical character of

his conclusion that the defining characteristic of cause and effect consists in the felt activity of habits of imagination, and he proceeds to answer a vain objection. "What! the efficacy of causes lie in the determination of the mind! As if causes did not operate entirely independent of the mind, and would not continue their operation, even though there was no mind existent to contemplate them. . . . Thought may well depend on causes for its operation, but not causes on thought. This is to reverse the order of nature, and make that secondary, which is really primary."[167] Hume would thus seem to express, and sharply enough, the retort of those who discern in the *Treatise* the assumption of causation in what he says about the inexplicable causes of impressions, about impressions as the causes of ideas, and about the force of association. How, then, without reversing the order of these assumptions, can Hume conclude the defining characteristic of causation to be the felt determination of habit?

The general answer to this question may be that, as at the outset Hume is giving a definition of cause and effect, so in conclusion he is describing the observed or felt nature of that relation. That impressions may have causes Hume does not deny. He says the "ultimate causes" of sense-impressions are, "in my opinion, perfectly inexplicable by human reason,"[84] and he finds the alleged necessity that they have a cause to be not demonstrable. Nor are his arguments that impressions are prior to and productive of ideas advanced as a denial that impressions are thus productive. And the attraction of association is also assumed and its origins are regarded as inexplicable. Yet this means that impressions, ideas, and the attraction of association are found to exist in constant conjunction, not in *necessary* connection. That the connection here should turn out upon examination to be the second nature of Pascal,* rather than the logical necessity of Malebranche, means that what has been called a necessary connection is in fact habitual; not that from this conclusion we may infer the non-existence of causes. For the fact that the rational necessity of causation is not to be demonstrated plainly does not imply that nothing in the nature of a cause can exist. If we do not know the laws of causality and causation to be true, neither do we know them to be false. Hence there is no reason, the contradictory of which would be inconceivable, why causes should be or should not be assumed.

Consistently with his denial of causation defined in terms of necessary connection, what Hume must explain is not the assumption of causes and effects, as in the case of association and habit, or

* *Pensées*, II, 93.

impression and idea; but rather in virtue of what it is that causal inference is felt to be ineluctable; or, in his language, the nature of the inference from impression to idea. This explanation having arrived at the conclusion that "necessity . . . is nothing but an internal impression of the mind, or a determination to carry our thoughts from one object to another,"[165] Hume properly insists so much as this to be all that can be meant by necessary connection or efficacy. "I am, indeed, ready to allow that there may be several qualities both in material and immaterial objects with which we are utterly unacquainted; and if we please to call these *power* or *efficacy*, it will be of little consequence to the world."[168] Though at liberty to speak at will about unknown powers and connections, in so doing we can rightly claim awareness of no more than our words and fancies.

Our actual knowledge of cause and effect may be stated in two definitions "which are only different, by their presenting a different view of the same object, and making us consider it either as a *philosophical* or as a *natural* relation; either as a comparison of two ideas, or as an association between them."[170] The philosophical relation comprehends the resembling contiguities and successions found in experience by comparison; and the natural relation comprehends this and the association also. The distinction between material, efficient, formal and final causes, and that between cause and occasion are thus meaningless; as is also the distinction between moral and physical necessity.*[171] The sole necessity in nature known to us is the determination of habit.

If Hume's sceptical analysis of cause and effect is to be distinguished from his theory of causal inference as that has so far been considered, it may now be asked whether that sceptical analysis is vitiated either by his copy theory of ideas or by his dogma that what is distinguishable is separable. The answer would seem to be fairly plain. Hume's main critical contention here is that neither by reason nor by sense-perception may the necessity of the causal relation be demonstrated. With respect to the principle of causality, we have noticed the first of his arguments to be based on his conception of the scope of intuitive certainty, and that the second one depends on the principle of his atomism. Nevertheless, the conclusions thus made out do not require for the validity of their import the truth of those assumptions. For the truth of the law of causality is surely not self-evident; and that its contradictory is conceivable also is plain. This Hume goes on to show, and with no reference to the requirements of his psychology, in exposing both the

* Cf. Boursier, *De l'action de Dieu sur les créatures.* (2 vols.) Paris, 1713.

fallacy in the proof of the law of causality advanced by Locke, and the verbal nature of the argument that every "effect" must have a cause. Hume's conclusion that the law of causality is neither intuitively certain nor demonstrable by apagogic reasoning thus may be apprehended apart from his own view of knowledge and of ideas as separable.

It is on this latter assumption that Hume denies the law of causation to be demonstrable by reason.[86, 87] The ideas of cause and effect being separable, there can be no contradiction in denying their necessary connection. Here again, however, Hume's conclusion is valid independently of the assumption on which he himself makes it out. For the contradictory of the law in question is conceivable. And in going on to show the uniformity of nature to be indemonstrable, Hume points out on the one hand that "we can at least conceive a change in the course of nature, which sufficiently proves that such a change is not absolutely impossible"; and, on the other, that the uniformity in question being the presupposition of probable reasoning, any attempt at its demonstration by induction could only beg the question.

The law of causation, being demonstrable by neither apagogic nor inductive reasoning, if demonstrable at all, will be so on the ground that necessary connection in fact is disclosed within sense-perception. Since Hume's failure to find that logical necessity obtains between the elements of sense-perceptions has been held to require his own analysis of experience, it may be well to consider briefly the fact that in other interests, and through a conception of experience not that of Hume, the same conclusion had been reached by three of "the Cartesians."

La Forge and Cordemoy were concerned to analyse the notion of efficient causation in order that those who would reject Descartes' philosophy because of his failure to explain the interaction of mind and body might see that, without recourse to the Deity, *no* case of interaction is explicable.* The central point that by sense-perception only impact, and no connection of any sort between bodies is to be found, was made out by La Forge† and elaborated by Cordemoy.‡ The further point that no connection between volitions and bodily movements is discoverable is touched upon by La Forge§ and developed at length by Cordemoy.|| What Hume summarily states as the Cartesian argument from the idea of extension, to the exclusion of power or efficacy from matter, is the

* *Traité de l'Esprit de l'Homme*, Ch. XVI, p. 242.
† Ibid., pp. 242, 243.
‡ *Traité sur le Discernement de l'Âme et du Corps*, pp. 99–105.
§ *Traité de l'Esprit de l'Homme*, pp. 80, 222, 266.
|| *Traité sur le Discernement de l'Âme et du Corps*, pp. 134, 135.

metaphysical explanation of this empirical state of affairs given by La Forge. Both from the fact that no logical connections are to be found in experience, and from this explanation of that fact, he concluded that God is the sole real cause.

By means of four "axioms," Cordemoy also advanced a metaphysical explanation both of his discovery that causal connections are to be found nowhere in experience, and of his conclusion that the vulgar belief in bodies as causes is a prejudice engendered by the constancy of their contiguity and succession in fact.* Bodies and souls are thus found to be not real causes but rather "occasions" for the application of the divine will.

At the outset of his examination of the idea of necessary connection,[158] Hume refers us to the *Recherche de la Vérité*, Book VI, Part II, chapter 3, wherein Malebranche states in summary fashion his own theory of Occasionalism. Perhaps it is because Hume goes on in his next sentence to give a free translation of Malebranche's indictment of certain scholastic views of causation, that he refers us also to "the illustrations" on the chapter in question. At any rate, these illustrations constitute the *XVe Éclaircissement* appended to the *Recherche*, wherein the author's Occasionalism is developed at length, and from which Hume's free

* *Traité sur le Discernement*, p. 105.

translation was made.* If this reference may not be taken for an acknowledgment of indebtedness, it surely puts beyond doubt Hume's acquaintance with a detailed analysis of causation by which his own conclusion that no *necessary* connections are to be found in matters of fact is elaborately made out.

Moreover, in his *Enquiry Concerning the Human Understanding*, Hume advances three arguments against the view that we are directly acquainted with a case of necessary connection in voluntary action, and two of these are arguments which had been urged by Malebranche who pointed out that the connection between a successful volition and the subsequent bodily movement is no less unknown than is that between any other successive events.† Hume's second argument here, that it is by experience alone that we learn which volitions are effective and which are not,† had been anticipated by La Forge and Cordemoy but was not advanced by Malebranche. Hume's third argument,‡ however, that we learn from anatomy the immediate consequences of volition to be not the movement of bodily members, but neural and muscular changes concerning which most men are

---

* *Recherche*, Edn. Bouillier, Vol. II, pp. 437, 438. In the English translation of the *Recherche* made by T. Taylor, M.A., of Magdalen College, Oxford, 1694 (2nd edn., 1700), the term "illustration" is used for "éclaircissement."

† *Enquiry*, Edn. Selby-Bigge, p. 65.   ‡ Ibid., p. 66.

quite ignorant, was argued by Malebranche in detail.

It will not be necessary for our purposes to enter into the arguments by which Malebranche sought to establish his theory of causation. In so far as they are negative, they converge on two main points; first, that the idea of extension excludes motion and hence causation from matter; and secondly, that neither by sense-perception nor in the experience of volition and bodily movement is an instance of necessary connection to be found.

Yet God is known to be omnipotent. Hence the positive conclusion that between the divine will and whatever happens there is known to be a necessary connection. This means that by definition God is the sole real cause. For "a real cause," Malebranche says, "is a cause between which and its effect, the mind perceives a necessary connection."* No such connection being found in experience, divine causation alone is real. Finite things are occasional causes. They afford God the opportunity (*l'occasion*) to diversify His activities, while remaining constant in the simplicity of His ways.

Malebranche took over from Cordemoy, to whom in this connection he refers† the discovery

---

* *Recherche*, Edn. Bouillier, Vol. II, pp. 64, 65.
† Ibid., Vol. I, p. 86.

that causal connections are to be found neither in sensory nor in volitional experience; a discovery that he converted into Hume's problem by his definition of the causal connection as necessary. In the interests of a theory about providence and grace, he developed a theory of causation. Of this theory one premise is the conclusion that necessary connections are not to be found in sense experience. The nature of Malebranche's theories about sense-perception would be difficult even to suggest in a few sentences. No one, however, who has attempted to follow their development out of the theories of vision and the *jugements naturels* of the *Recherche*, into the *révélations naturelles* of the *Entretiens Métaphysiques*, will want to compare them concretely with the doctrine of impressions and ideas. Neither the interests of the Cartesians, La Forge, Cordemoy, and Malebranche, in the problem of causation, nor their attempts (where made) to analyse experience, were those of Hume. Yet the one conclusion for which Hume is perhaps best known is common to them all.

II

At the outset of his *Scepticism with regard to the senses*, Hume writes: "We may well ask, *What causes induce us to believe in the existence of body?* but it is vain to ask, *Whether there be body*

95

or not? That is a point, which we must take for granted in all our reasonings."[187] What the nature of this "body" is, we shall ask in Chapter IV. Here the point to be emphasized is that throughout his analysis of our belief in an external world, Hume takes for granted the existence of body in some sense of that term. He thus goes directly on to say, "The subject, then, of our present enquiry is concerning the *causes* which induce us to believe in the existence of body."[187, 188] Hume's scepticism with regard to the senses is concerned not with the existence of matter, but with the causes of a belief which he finds can be demonstrated neither by reason nor by sense-perception.

The uncritical opinion about material existence is a belief in the continued existence of things distinct from present perception. Continued existence implies independent existence. From this Hume (uncritically) infers the truth of the converse. He therefore asserts that an understanding of the causes of our belief either in continued or in independent existence will explain the causes of our belief in both. The "absurdity" of an external existence "specifically different" from our perceptions having already been shown,* the causes of our belief, whether in continued or independent existence, are to be sought for within "the *senses, reason*, or the *imagination*."[188]

* See above, p. 54.

96

A continued existence unperceived cannot in the nature of the case be perceived. Only the independent existence of things may therefore be revealed by the senses. Yet our senses "convey to us nothing but a single perception, and never give us the least intimation of anything beyond."[189] The impression of "a double existence" must then be suggested by "a kind of fallacy and illusion." This will derive not from the sense-perceptions themselves, but from "their relations and situation."[189] It may appear that sense-perceptions plainly are situated outside ourselves. Were this the case, not only they but also ourselves would be obvious for comparison by our senses.[189] Yet only by "the most profound metaphysics" can a satisfactory theory of the self be made out; and no such theory is present in the operations of the senses.[189, 190]

It is plain also that perceptions can no more be deceptive in their relations than in themselves. "For since all actions and sensations of the mind are known to us by consciousness, they must necessarily appear in every particular what they are, and be what they appear."[190] Since there is no appearance of independent existence either as "represented" by or as original in sense-perception, no such independence is perceived by the senses.

It is furthermore plain that we cannot compare our bodies with our sense-perceptions thus to discover the independent existence of the latter.[191] For it is in and through our sense-perceptions that what we regard as our body appears. It is therefore as difficult to explain why a corporeal existence should be ascribed to those perceptions as why it should not be attributed to others. And even though this should be explained, the question of the independent existence of sense-perceptions ("objects") would remain. To this Hume adds that since "sounds, and tastes, and smells, though commonly regarded by the mind as continued independent qualities, appear not to have any existence in extension,"[191] they cannot appear as external existences. The distinction between primary and secondary qualities is not disclosed by the senses, but is the result of theory and therefore falls outside of the present question.

In his examination *Of the Modern Philosophy*, however, Hume returns to the distinction between primary and secondary qualities. To this modern attempt at reconciling observed change with a belief in permanence, he thinks many objections may be made. The one to which he will confine himself, however, is that "instead of explaining the operations of external objects by its means, we utterly annihilate all these objects, and reduce ourselves to the opinions of the most extravagant scepticism concerning them."[227, 228] Thus he proceeds to urge that the primary qualities may not be known in separation from the secondary.

Since motion must be that of a body, motion is not imaginable apart from extension and solidity. Extension is not found apart from colour. Hence extension may not be known apart from that quality. Again, solidity must be that of bodies; and of bodies the secondary qualities afford no idea. As for the secondary quality of hardness, that feeling is one thing, whereas solidity itself is another.[230] "Our modern philosophy, therefore, leaves us no just nor satisfactory idea of solidity; nor consequently of matter."[229] Apart from both colour and hardness, no one of "the primary qualities chiefly insisted on"[228] may be so much as imagined. The distinction in question, therefore, would put beyond the possible content of belief the very qualities whose independent and permanent existence it was designed to explain.

Because the senses "cannot operate beyond the extent in which they really operate,"[191] continued existence is not discoverable by the senses. Distinct existence can appear neither "as represented nor as original"; not as a representation, for that would be the appearance of an image and what it represents in one; and not directly, for what does appear in sense-perception is exhausted in the very perceptions themselves. Any suggestion by the senses of continued or independent existence would be "fallacy and illusion." Yet what perceptions are in every particular fully appears as they occur. In this appearance there is no suggestion of distinct existence. Therefore, no such illusion may originate with the *senses*.

Hence Hume concludes "with certainty" that the causes sought for are not to be found in sense-perception. That they are not rational, Hume thinks is shown by the fact that in positing the existence of bodies we consult neither our own reasonings nor the theories of the philosophers.[193] Since philosophy informs us that every appearance "is nothing but a perception," whereas "the vulgar confound perceptions and objects," philosophical theory and common opinion are here in contradiction. Referring now to a point made further on in concluding his positive theory of belief in material substance, Hume says that even though bodies are not identified with perceptions, but are assumed to have a separate reality, their existence may not be inferred from the appearance of perceptions.

Thus, in order to show that his conclusions regarding the causes in question have "no primary recommendation" to reason,[212] Hume reminds us that from present perceptions the existence of something not present may be inferred only in virtue of the natural relation of cause and effect. Constant conjunction in experience being a condition of the existence of this relation, it cannot hold between perceptions and something which *ex hypothesi* lies beyond all experience. The existence of bodies, therefore, may not be inferred from the existence of such perceptions as are assumed to be their effects.

Had Hume, in Section 6 of Part I, not asked those philosophers who imagine that we have clear ideas of substance about the impression from which such ideas could be derived, he might have opened his scepticism with regard to the senses with an argument to the conclusion that in fact we have no image of this substance of the philosophers. This, we have noticed, he does not do. Although there is to be found no impression of an extended substratum, the belief in an external world nevertheless remains to be explained on the experimental method by the discovery of its causes.

Thus at the outset of his scepticism regarding the senses, Hume may assume the absence of any idea of body to have been established in Section 6 of Part I. The subject of his enquiry will then be as to what causes induce us to believe in the existence of something we cannot picture in imagination. Throughout this section the synonymous use of perception and object is annoyingly constant. It may nevertheless be urged that had

Hume been consistent here with his first principle, he would have looked for impressions from which ideas of continued and independent existence respectively might be derived. This would be to assume that Hume thought of "continued existence" and "independent existence" as names of impressions that might be found. And for this there would appear to be no evidence. Existence is for Hume in no case a distinguishable characteristic of actual perceptions. *Continued* existence is therefore looked for as though *it* might be a characteristic of perceptions, objects or impressions, but not an impression or object or perception in its own right. Such is also the case with *independent* existence. Even though it be assumed that here Hume ought to have written of impressions of the senses, rather than of "the senses" or "objects" or "perceptions," it still does not follow that, consistently with his denial of any idea of existence, he could have applied his first principle in his search for the causes in question in sense-perception. For to have done so would have been to assume that there might be *ideas* of continued and independent *existence*.

Hume's arguments to his conclusion that the distinct existence of objects is not present to the senses leave much to be desired. His inference that because some perceptions, such as pains, are not external, all perceptions are internal, is plainly vicious. Again, he begs the question in taking it for granted that our bodies are no more than perceptions; and he uncritically assumes that *apparent* distance is not an object of vision. Yet it would seem to be clear that what is *ex hypothesi* "represented" cannot itself be present in its alleged representation. Since the distinct existence in question is that of something independent of the perceptions or objects themselves, it could hardly fall within them there to be exhibited, and hence is not to be found. With regard to continued existence, plainly an existent not perceived is *ipso facto* not perceived continuously.

In his analysis of personal identity Hume relies on his first principle.[251] The substance in question being something "simple and continued," its idea would be derived from an impression which remained invariable throughout the course of our lives; and plainly no such impression is to be found. This argument plainly fails to show that a transitory act of introspection *might* not discover spiritual substance and recognize it as such. In accordance with his doctrine of impressions and ideas, Hume here assumes not only that the idea in question must be a copy, but also that the impression must be as continuous in existence as would be the alleged substance.

The validity of his position here thus depends on the fact that "when I enter most intimately into what I call *myself*," Hume finds no more than "some particular perception or other."[252] That this is a question of fact, Hume readily acknowledges. If, "upon serious and unprejudiced reflection," anyone thinks he introspects anything other than perceptions, Hume can only agree "that he may be in the right as well as I, and that we are essentially different in this particular."[252] But Hume thinks "metaphysicians of this kind" may be disregarded, and the conclusion drawn that the generality of mankind are "nothing but a bundle or collection of different perceptions."[252] The importance of the term "bundle" in this context will appear in connection with Hume's constructive theory of the self.

One of the metaphysicians whom Hume sets apart from this conclusion concerning the generality of mankind may have been Malebranche. The "intimate consciousness" of the self that Hume fails to find would then be his translation of the "sentiment intérieur" Malebranche thought us to have of the existence, but not of the essence, of the self. And if Hume did not skip the *XIe* on his way to the *XVe Éclaircissement* of the *Recherche*, he would have been acquainted with a view on which a denial of all knowledge of spiritual substance in and through sensuous consciousness is argued in detail.

It was Malebranche's conviction that God

would not reveal the idea of the soul because by the contemplation of its beauty men would be distracted from the performance even of their plainest duties. Descartes must therefore have been mistaken in his conclusion that the nature of thought is better known than is anything else. In fact, "the Cartesians themselves" conclude that the sense qualities belong to thought not because they find this to be so by an inspection of the soul, but in virtue of the exclusion of these qualities from matter. This in itself shows that Descartes and his followers here have no clear idea of the soul. It is moreover plain that in no case of sensuous consciousness will more than the inclinations, passions or images of sense and imagination present be revealed. Thus, "even though we are actually feeling pain, or seeing a colour, we cannot discover by inspection that these qualities belong to the soul."* Nothing in the presence of a sensuously conscious state reveals anything beyond itself. Hence the substance of the soul—the pure understanding—may not be discovered by introspection, of which the object, for Malebranche, would not have been an impression.

* *Recherche,* Edn. Bouillier, Vol. II, p. 403. Cf. Vol. I, p. 443. Also *Méditations Chrétiennes,* IX, 15.

CHAPTER III

Causal Inference

THE general nature of belief having been defined, its causes remain to be ascertained. This Hume proceeds to do in Section 8 of Part III: *Of the causes of belief.* The origins of simple and complex ideas having been examined in Part I, and the causes of impressions being beyond our reach, the one element of the definition of belief which is yet to be examined is that of association. In illustrating in this connection the workings of association, Hume is not concerned further to establish resemblance, contiguity, and cause and effect as natural relations, but rather to bring out the effect of those relations on the ideas which are evoked by their force.[98]

Accordingly, he points out that "the appearance" of a picture of an absent friend, in virtue of the resemblance presented, evokes an idea which is enlivened by that resemblance. Contiguity, though a natural relation, is the cause of an added liveliness in the idea evoked only when that idea is of something not too far distant in space or time from the perception present.* And

* "The thinking on any object readily transports the mind to what is contiguous; but 'tis only the actual presence of an object that transports it with a superior vivacity. When I am a few miles

in view of the reverence of the superstitious for the relics of saints, the effect of causation in enlivening ideas thus evoked is also not to be doubted.

Nevertheless, Hume will further treat of the matter "as a question in natural philosophy," to be decided "by experience and observation."[101] Accordingly, he first observes that "a single perception, limited to the present moment,"[102] is a mere impression, suggesting nothing beyond itself. We thus see that a belief cannot consist of an impression alone. "Only after repeated experience" of "its usual consequences" are we able to infer in idea the consequence of a present impression.

Hume next observes that the transition from impression to idea "arises immediately" without the intervention of any "new [as distinguished from repeated] operation of the reason or imagination."[102] He can be certain of this because, in the occurrence of his own beliefs, he finds no such "new" operation. That being so, and since whatever "proceeds from a past repetition, without any new reasoning or conclusion" is what we mean by custom,[102] we may conclude custom to be the origin of all belief that is consequent upon a present impression.

from home, whatever relates to it touches me more nearly than when I am two hundred leagues distant; though even at that distance the reflecting on anything in the neighbourhood of my friends and family naturally produces an idea of them."[100]

In what he now advances as a "third set of experiments,"[103] Hume observes that in an association between ideas there is no "belief or persuasion." Custom, then, is not enough. That the idea evoked by association may have the added force and vivacity characteristic of belief, an actual impression is required.

Each one of the three elements defined is thus shown to be necessary to the constitution of belief. Although the natural relations of resemblance, contiguity, and cause and effect enliven the ideas they evoke, that the vivacity of belief, rather than a mere association of ideas, may result, the actual operation of these customs must be provoked by a present impression. And since to the degree to which fancies are "perfect ideas," they are independent of the natural relations, the ideal content of belief will be never fancies but always ideas lively in virtue of their association with an impression.

Thus having established it "as a general maxim in the science of human nature" that an impression not only evokes ideas by association, *"but likewise communicates to them a share of its force and vivacity,"*[98] Hume goes on to raise two questions concerning his definition of belief. The first of these is how the fact that we sometimes recognize a cause "merely by one experiment" is to be explained.[104] Since constant conjunction is a condition of the natural relation of cause and effect, it may seem that in all cases where only one conjunction has occurred no causal inference can arise. But this would be to forget that "cause" and "effect" alike are terms in discourse associated at once with habits and with the images evoked by the occurrence of those terms. Upon the appearance of a novel conjunction which in certain respects resembles past perceptions habitually designated cause and effect, "we transfer," "either *expressly* or *tacitly*, either *directly* or *indirectly*," that designation to the novel conjunction.[105] The force of the natural relation of cause and effect, itself engendered in imagination by "many millions" of experiences of conjunction, is transferred to the novel conjunction because of the resemblance of that conjunction with those past. The "transfer" is thus a case of association by resemblance. Whether this association is "tacit," or overt, will depend on the degree of "perfection" of the custom that is one of its terms. Thus, in accordance with his theory of abstract ideas, Hume observes, "that in all the most established and uniform conjunctions of causes and effects, such as those of gravity, impulse, solidity, etc., the mind never carries its view expressly to consider any past experience."[104] For, as we have noticed, the more solid the habit, the less the felt need that a definite image to accompany the name associated with such a custom should be evoked. Where the character of a novel conjunction resembles the content of a strongly established habit, that conjunction will without hesitation be designated cause and effect. Where the resemblance is to the tangle of habits which arise from "contrarieties" in experience, the association will be not direct and undoubted; it will be felt as "probable."

The second question which Hume here raises concerns the fact that a sufficiently lively idea may on occasion instigate a belief. His example is that of an idea "of which I have forgot the correspondent impression,"[105] and from which he yet is "able to conclude . . . that such an impression did once exist."[106] But whence the force of such a conclusion? Hume answers "very readily" that the force derives from the initial idea. "For as this idea is not here considered as the representation of any absent object, but as a real perception in the mind, of which we are intimately conscious, it must be able to bestow on whatever is related to it the same quality, call it *firmness, or solidity, or force, or vivacity*, with which the mind reflects upon it, and is assured of its present existence."[106] This is difficult to reconcile with Hume's previous conclusion that no mere association of ideas can give rise to belief.

Yet his view now is that a sufficiently lively idea may evoke another image and communicate to it a share of its own force and vivacity. In such cases the idea "supplies the place of an impression, and is entirely the same, so far as regards our present purpose,"[106] which is to discover the causes of belief.

Here again the distinction between impressions and ideas fails to hold. As upon occasion an image may not be distinguishable from an impression, and as in no particular case the "impressions" of memory can be distinguished with assurance from the impressions of sensation, so now an idea, in virtue of its own vivacity, may have the effect in belief of an impression. The assurance that in any given case a belief derives from sense-experience is thus eliminated. The determinations of habit, ranging in force (as we shall see) from the strength of felt proofs to the weakness of felt possibilities, alone remain to control the character of beliefs.

Hume now proceeds (in Section 9) to consider "the effects of other relations and other habits" on belief. Here it is his chief contention that transitive inference, or belief in the existence of things absent, can be effected not by the natural relations of resemblance and contiguity, but only by that of cause and effect.[107] In order to make this out Hume anticipates briefly in an enigmatic paragraph something of his theory of belief in things.

It will be evident that memories, because of their superior force, are of more moment in the mind than are its fancies.[107, 108] Of such forceful images "a kind of system" is formed. This system, because it is in "every particular" associated with present impressions, "we are pleased to call a *reality*."[108]

Along with this first system of memory and sense imagery, "there is another connected by custom, or if you will, by the relation of cause or effect . . ." to the first.[108] The ideas evoked by impressions from this second system, the mind "feels that it is in a manner necessarily determined to view . . ." because the customs which constitute this second system are firmly established.[108] Therefore the mind forms these ideas "into a new system, which it likewise dignifies with the title of *realities*."[108] Of these two systems, the first is "the object of the memory and senses; the second of the judgment."[108]

A "*reality*" actually present thus consists of a system of memories associated in "every particular" with "present impressions."[108] The associated constituents of such objects being exhaustively mnemonic and sensory in nature, there is involved no belief in the existence of a similar object not then present. Only the "realities"

formed in virtue of the second system, that of
habits of causal inference, are believed to represent
absent objects. Thus, Hume's next paragraph
here opens with the following explanation: "It is
this latter principle ['judgment'] which peoples
the world, and brings us acquainted with such
existences, as by their removal in time and place,
lie beyond the reach of the senses and memory.
By means of it I paint the universe in my
imagination, and fix my attention on any part of
it I please."[108] Whereas the realities which consist
of the system of memories and sense-impressions
are objects wholly present and called things, a
reality resulting from a system of habits of causal
inference is believed to represent, but not itself
to *be* an existing thing.

The difference between belief in the existence
of realities present, and belief in their existence
as represented by inference, thus being explained,
Hume proceeds directly to consider the effects of
adventitious associations by resemblance and contiguity on beliefs of the latter sort. A poet may
indeed enliven his reverie about the Elysian fields
by gazing upon a beautiful meadow; and, by
imagining himself to be in those regions, he may
further enliven his dreams by "the feigned
contiguity."[109] Although such arbitrary and
adventitious associations may enliven belief in the
existence of things pictured in imagination as the

result of causal inference, yet being thus capricious, they can have little of the force of established habits of causal inference. In all such cases "there is no manner of necessity for the mind to feign any resembling and contiguous objects; and if it feigns such, there is as little necessity for it always to confine itself to the same, without any difference or variation. And indeed such a fiction is founded on so little reason that nothing but pure *caprice* can determine the mind to form it; and that principle being fluctuating and uncertain, it is impossible it can ever operate with any considerable degree of force and constancy."[109] The caprices of reverie may by association enliven normal beliefs. But in view of their arbitrary freedom it is not to be feared that reveries ever could replace in belief the effects of established custom.

It is thus at this point that Hume considers the effects of fancy on belief. His language sometimes suggests a fancy to be a quite fugacious image. This is to say, however, that usually such unaccountable ideas are associated loosely with the habits of the imagination, not that to be a fancy is necessarily to have no associations at all. The extent to which an idea is without associations is the extent to which it is free and a fancy. The two extremes here are, on the one hand, that of an idea isolated by the absence of any associations whatever, and on the other, that of an idea which contributes to constitute a perfect habit in imagination. As ideas approach in freedom the first extreme, they are evoked the more capriciously, being the less controlled by habitual associations. Hence their association with beliefs will be "fluctuating and uncertain," and without "any considerable degree of force and constancy."[109] At the other extreme, ideas will be the firmly associated contents of established customs or habits in imagination. Such ideas when associated with impressions will constitute beliefs devoid of doubt.

After illustrating "the influence of belief" in Section 10, Hume turns in the next section to "the probability of chances." Since "in common discourse we readily affirm, that many arguments from causation exceed probability, and may be received as a superior kind of evidence,"[124] Hume will not follow those philosophers who distinguish only knowledge and probability, and hence are obliged to consider as a species of the latter all arguments from cause and effect. Rather he will distinguish knowledge, proofs, and probabilities. Knowledge, he repeats, derives from a comparison of ideas; proofs are "those arguments, which are derived from the relation of cause and effect, and which are entirely free from doubt . . .";[124] probabilities, on the contrary, are inferences whose conclusions are felt to be uncertain. The probability of causes is to be distinguished from, and is considered after, the probability of chances.

The natural relation of cause and effect so determines the order of our ideas in some one particular way "that we cannot without a sensible violence survey them in any other."[125] Chance is the negation of this determination. It is not a relation or quality of any sort, but "is merely the negation of a cause."[125] Chance, therefore, is not something that in any way influences the mind; "and it is essential to it, to leave the imagination perfectly indifferent, either to consider the existence or non-existence of that object, which is regarded as contingent."[125] This indifference, or absence of causal determination in the imagination, being what "chance" means, a superiority in chances cannot be due to any one mere chance as opposed to any other. For all chances are as such indifferent. A superiority in chance must then be due to the superiority of the number of chances of a given set.

Since a felt indifference to habits of causal inference is the nature of chance, no multiplication in the number of chances could begin to move the imagination to make an inference. Hence the requirement of "supposing a mixture of causes among the chances, and a conjunction of necessity in some particulars, with a total indifference in others."[125, 126] Only on the assumption that a die thrown will at once fall and remain the same throughout the process can it be inferred that as a result of the throw one side alone of that die will turn up.

Were the six surfaces of the die without pips, that any one of these blank surfaces may turn up would exhaust the range of inference in that case. Inference to a felt superiority in chances would arise in the case of Hume's example, where a die thrown has four sides marked with one set of pips, the other two sides being marked with another set. Here it is expected that one alone of these sides will turn up. Since the sides as surfaces are indifferent, this expectation "directs us to the whole six sides after such a manner as to divide its force equally among them."[129] Thus we notice two of the three causes of conjectural inference. First, there is the operation of those habits of inference which determine the initial expectation. Secondly, there is the division of this expectation indifferently with respect to the six surfaces of the die. Because these surfaces as such are indifferent, no one of them will be preferred in expectation to any other. This means, in Hume's view, that the initial expectation is given indifferently or "equally" to each one of the sides. Hence, in the act of considering the six sides, the initial expectation divides itself into six equal amounts.

Considering now the sides in their character as marked, Hume's question is how the superiority in the number of sides marked with one set of pips can determine us to favour the chances of any one of those sides.[129, 130]

His answer is that of the six equal amounts of expectation initially given indifferently to the six surfaces, four are now given to any one of the four sides marked with the same set of pips. These "must re-unite in that one figure, and become stronger and more forcible by that union."[130] There being now felt not six equal units of impulse, but four and two units respectively, the union of the four impulses will constitute an anticipation stronger than that effected by the union of the two impulses remaining. The two anticipations thus constituted will conflict, with the result that "the inferior destroys the superior, as far as its strength goes."[130] Thus Hume explains the third cause of probable inference; namely, the reunion in different amounts of the initially equal units of expectation.

In his explicit account here of felt chances, Hume is assuming (1) that the initial impulse of expectation has a certain amount of force; (2) that this may be indifferently (equally) or differently (unequally) divided; and (3) that the resulting units of force may reunite so as to form equal or unequal amounts of force in anticipation. There

118

is, however, in his account of probable inference nothing inconsistent with his conclusion that repetition "neither discovers nor produces" anything new in perception. Were all six sides of the die marked differently, or were all marked the same, no one side could be favoured in expectation. But because of the *absence* of difference in the marking of two sides, of the six impulses initially distributed indifferently over the six surfaces, four unite on the identical marking of the four sides, two on that of the two sides. This union thus results not from any property or accident of the character or number of the sets of pips, but rather from an absence of difference in the four and two sets of pips respectively.

With regard to the operation of habits of causal inference, Hume observes, "When we follow only the habitual determination of the mind, we make the transition without any reflection, and interpose not a moment's delay betwixt the view of one object and the belief of that which is often found to attend it. As the custom depends not upon any deliberation, it operates immediately, without allowing any time for reflection."[133] Such is the case with habits that are full and perfect, like that of referring recollections into the future. But commonly, inferences are made concerning irregularities in events. These are not to be explained as the work of repetition in habits of imagination. For in such cases repetition is not expected. Therefore more than mere repetition in habit must be involved in all inferences that result not in ineluctable beliefs in causes and effects, but rather in their probability.

Since these probable inferences are not matters of mnemonic repetition associated with present impressions, they arise from habit not directly but in an "oblique manner." This results from a conflict among associations corresponding to the contrariety in events. All causal inference is controlled by the habit of referring past experience into the future.[134] But when past experiences "of a contrary nature" are recalled, the force of that habit is not united on any one object, but is diffused over the variety of images present. The initial impulse of the habit, therefore, "is here broke into pieces, and diffuses itself over all those images, of which each partakes an equal share of that force and vivacity that is derived from the impulse."[134] In virtue of this equal division of the impulse, each one of the images present is felt with equal force. Hence we believe indifferently in the recurrence of any one of the events recollected. In virtue of the same motive, we believe also that with respect to one another these events will recur in the same order as before. By long observation, a lighthouse-keeper finds that out of twenty ships which put to sea, one is always lost. Upon witnessing the sailings of twenty ships, his past experience will be referred to the future in the felt conviction that only nineteen ships will return. In this case, which would be that of the operation of an established habit, the images "remain in their *first form,* and preserve their first proportions."[134] The habit of expecting the return of nineteen and the loss of one of the ships will not be "broke up" or altered in any way in the course of its operation.

But whenever a single belief derives from a contrariety of past events, the ideas then involved are not merely repeated. For in this case the ideas will be images not of uniform recurrences, but of multiform events. The habitual impulse to refer the past into the future will be initially divided indifferently among the various incoherent images. Of these let us suppose there are eighteen, in ten of which there is an absence of difference in one respect, whereas in eight there is an absence of difference in another. Ten units of impulse will unite on an idea of the first sort, while eight unite on an idea of the second. "This operation of the mind has been so fully explained in treating of the probability of chance, that I need not here endeavour to render it more intelligible."[135] Hume concludes this paragraph with the explanation that, as we can now see, what he has said about the probability of chances is applicable also to belief in the probability of causes.[135]

When belief results from the operation of a single habit, there is then no question of a felt probability: the repetition of past causes and effects is assumed with conviction. Such conviction will result from the operation of the habitual impulse to refer recollections into the future only when, as in the case of the twenty ships, there is no conflict among habits in imagination. Whenever any such conflict arises, the impulse into the future is then "broke up" and initially diffused indifferently over the conflicting images. This means that initially the images are no less indifferent with respect to our expectation than are the sides of the die as surfaces. But considered in point of their agreement, or lack of difference, in certain respects the images will be like the marked sides of the die, and units of impulse will unite on a typical image to a number which will be in each case that of the images of that type.

Belief in the probability of causes will thus result not from the operation of a single habit of causal inference, but rather from a conflict among habits engendered by a "contrariety of experiments."[135] The fact that most causal inferences are of this latter sort, Hume emphasizes; and this may account for his going on further to justify views which he thinks to have made out fully in his account of the probability of chances. Accordingly he first observes that no probability can be so great as to exclude all contrary possibilities; for otherwise the case would be a certainty. He then asserts that the component parts of this probability and possibility "are of the same nature and differ in number only," not in kind.[136] For as chances as such are equally indifferent, just so ideas of causes as such are of the "same weight," and "it is only a superior number of them, which can throw the balance on any side."[136] Ideas of causes will be felt indifferently as mere chances so long as the impulse into the future is divided among them indifferently. But that impulse will find in some of the ideas present an absence of difference in certain respects, and its scattered impulses to the number of those ideas will reunite on any one of them. The idea thus believed probably to represent a cause will be that on which the largest number of impulses concur, while the remaining impulses reunite to constitute the felt force of a possibility.

Felt proof and mere chance are the two extremes at both of which felt probability disappears. Beliefs resulting from established and coherent habits of causal inference will be proofs: the existence of the cause or effect as represented in such beliefs will be posited with conviction. For unlike beliefs in the probability of causes and effects, which arise from conflicting habits, in the formation of proofs the impulse into the future is neither initially nor in the result apportioned among conflicting ideas. Throughout the inference to a felt proof the impulse into the future concentrates on ideas derived from a group of coherent habits. Hence the single-minded conviction of such beliefs as are felt proofs.

At the other extreme of bare chance all feeling of conviction is absent. For chance is the negation of the source of conviction in transitive inference; viz. the natural relation of cause and effect.

Ideas of causes may be entertained as mere chances. This is the case when they are felt as having the same weight of expectancy, with the impulse into the future distributed equally among them. So regarded as chances, ideas of causes are taken in isolation; taken quite apart from their association within habits of causal inference of which *chance* is the *negation*. It is thus only when entertained as mere chances that ideas of causes and effects are taken to exist without their associations within imagination.

It is clearly Hume's view, not only for the purpose of expounding the probability of causes, but also in fact, that every idea of a cause or effect may be regarded as a mere chance. "Every past experiment may be considered as a kind of chance; it being uncertain to us, whether the object will exist conformable to one experiment or another: and for this reason everything that has been said on the one subject is applicable to both."[135] Considered simply in itself, every "past experiment has the same weight."[136] It is only in virtue of its association within a habit in imagination, of which it will be an image-content, that the idea of a cause or an effect will be not entertained as a mere chance, but felt to be a probability.

The difference between ideas entertained indifferently as chances and the same ideas so associated as to be probable beliefs is again plain in the first of the three stages of Hume's analysis of the probability of chances. It will be recalled that he first points out that from a mere chance no inference can be drawn. In the situation that is the throwing of a die there must be involved at least one habit of causal inference. Some of the ideas then present must be felt not as quite detached, but as associated with a habit in imagination. This habit will be that one which, in virtue of its associations with the present situation, will be aroused by the throw of a die. Hence by that habit of which they are image-content the ideas in question will be associated within the present situation. This is to say that these ideas of causes and effects will be associated with that sensory-mnemonic "system" which is here the actual "reality"; viz. the situation of the die as thrown. These ideas will constitute the second "system" in their association with the first: they will be an expectant belief that the causes which they represent are realities to ensue in the situation.

Though any image, being distinct, may be separated from its associations, an image as separate will be a content of no inference or belief. Such an image may be called in Hume's terms either a mere fancy or a chance; the former because mere fancies are ideas without associations; the latter because the separation of the idea from all habits of inference negates with respect to it the force of causal inference.

Ideas of causes and effects will be regarded as bare chances when they are felt in separation from, or as indifferent to, the habits in imagination of which they are the contents. We have noticed that in Hume's analysis of the probability of causes, such ideas are at one stage in the development of probabilities felt indifferently as chances. At the initial stage the ideas are so many images, amongst which the impulse into the future is equally divided. Without benefit of prejudice, this conception of the incipience of felt probabilities would hardly be identified with the nature of an actual belief in causes and effects as probable. The image-content of these beliefs will be not felt chances, indifferent to any custom whatever, but rather constituents of felt probabilities. Since these beliefs will be not isolated ideas or mere fancies, their existence is not the occurrence of "atomic" ideas.

It is, moreover, Hume's view that in the development of probabilities into proofs the stages are normally not discriminated. "As the habit, which produces the association, arises from the frequent conjunction of objects, it must arrive at its perfection by degrees, and must acquire new force from each instance that falls under our observation. The first instance has little or no force: the second makes some addition to it: the third becomes still more sensible; and it is by these slow steps, that our judgment arrives at a full assurance. But before it attains this pitch of perfection, it passes through several inferior degrees, and in all of them is only to be esteemed a presumption or probability. The gradation, therefore, from probabilities to proofs is in many cases insensible; and the difference betwixt these kinds of evidence is more easily perceived in the remote degrees, than in the near and contiguous."[130, 131] And Hume goes on to say that, although the probability of causes is genetically prior to the existence of proofs, "yet no one, who is arrived at the age of maturity, can any longer be acquainted with it."[131] Hume's view of the matter would thus appear to be that the components of these beliefs appear in actual experience not as isolated ideas, associations, and impressions, but rather as the syntheses or "systems" which beliefs are in his view. It is only at the extremes of chance and proof that the components of probable beliefs are easily distinguished by analysis. In mature experience such distinctions do not appear at all. For the experience of mature persons is not itself the analysis by which Hume seeks to elucidate the components of felt probabilities and proofs. Such experience will be rather those sensory-mnemonic "systems" which are the objects of the senses, and those "systems" which are felt probabilities and proofs; neither of which is an isolated impression, association, or idea.

Although beliefs in causes as probable are genetically prior to beliefs in them as inevitable, genetically prior to probable beliefs are, on the one hand, mere impressions and mere ideas, and, on the other, the gentle force of association. For these are the elements of belief. Now if it be agreed that Hume's conception of the synthesis of ideas by association to form habits or customs at least equals in its importance for his theory of the understanding his analysis of the perceptions of the mind, it must be admitted that for him a perception is not properly identified with either one of its species, but is rather an *habitual association* of ideas and impressions. In the existence of a belief of any sort, there is always at the least "a lively idea associated with a present impression," never a bare impression or idea in isolation. That any such isolated state of consciousness might exist, all associations would have to be eliminated, thus negating causal inference and achieving the bare indifference of mere chance. In view of Hume's theory of belief, this would hardly seem to be his conception of unanalysed experience. That he analyses the perceptions of the mind into ideas associated with impressions does not imply that the terms of this analysis are by Hume assumed to exist normally in isolation. In the light of his constructive theory of causal inference, it is rather to be concluded that, except for fancies and bare chances, a perception of the mind consists of ideas habitually associated with certain impressions; which is by definition the nature of belief.

CHAPTER IV

Belief in Substance

I

SINCE our belief in the continued existence of things can be demonstrated neither by sense-perception nor by reason, "that opinion must be entirely owing to the *Imagination*: which must now be the subject of our enquiry."[193] Accordingly, in the next paragraph, Hume opens his enquiry into the nature and causes of belief in continued existence. And the first sentences of this paragraph make it plain that it is with the continued existence of impressions that he is concerned. For he affirms that all impressions are and appear as "internal and perishing existences";[194] that (perception and reason being excluded) "the notion of their distinct and continued existence must arise from a concurrence of some of their qualities with the qualities of the imagination," and that since only some impressions are believed to have a continued existence, that belief "must arise from certain qualities peculiar to some impressions."[194]

Neither involuntariness (as Locke had thought to be the case) nor superior force and vivacity cause us to believe in the independent existence of certain impressions as opposed to others; for what is less voluntary and more forceful than a twinge of pain? The first of the "qualities" in question to be found "after a little examination" is the "*constancy*" of such impressions as are believed to have a continued existence. "Those mountains, and houses, and trees, which lie at present under my eye, have always appeared to me in the same order; and when I lose sight of them by shutting my eyes or turning my head, I soon after find them return on me without the least alteration."[194] Or, negatively, my present perception is such as to evoke no recollection of it as different. But mere repetition in the order and content of perceptions cannot explain our belief in their continued existence. For things often change both in the order and character of their perceived qualities. "But here it is observable, that even in these changes they preserve a *coherence*, and have a regular dependence on each other; which is the foundation of a kind of reasoning from causation, and produces the opinion of their continued existence."[195] The "constancy" in question is that of the contents of the "first system" already referred to; viz. that of the memory and the senses. Since this system excludes both outright fancies, and those impressions and ideas whose difference prevents their being associated with its own contents, it

131

contains only repeated resemblances in habitual association. Hence the alterations or differences in perceived things cannot be accounted for by the constancy of the system of the memory and senses. Yet these alterations are adjusted in imagination to the repeated memories and sense-impressions by "a kind of inference from causation," as is illustrated by Hume's account of the entry of the porter bearing a letter.

Seated in his chamber, his memory recalls experiences past, while he is aware also of those then present; "but then this information extends not beyond their past existence, nor do either my senses or memory give any testimony to the continuance of their being."[196] But on hearing the noise of his door being opened, and seeing the porter enter bearing a letter, he infers the continued existence of his door, his stairway, and of "posts and ferries"; because, with regard to that particular noise, the appearance of a person in his chamber, and the transportation of letters, such habits of causal inference have been formed in him.[196] The sound heard, the porter and the letter appearing, with their attendant memories, give Hume no assurance of anything beyond themselves. Yet, because these appearances and memories actuate the operation of habits associated with them, Hume infers the continued existence of such causes as are the condition of the repetition of these appearances. Thus it is that sensory and mnemonic experience is extended in accordance with rules existing as habits of imagination. This is also the case where present impressions evoke memories of experiences resembling those present in the main but different from them in part. The alteration in the present experience will then be explained by inferences to those causes which have been associated with like changes in the past. When Hume returns to his study after an hour's absence, he finds that his fire has burned down. "But then I am accustomed in other instances to see a like alteration produced in a like time, whether I am present or absent, near or remote. This coherence, therefore, in their changes is one of the characteristics of external objects, as well as their constancy.'[195] Unusual or non-coherent changes would be associated with no habits in imagination. Therefore they could not be explained as coherent with the thing thus altered.

In order to explain why we believe objects to remain the same despite apparent alterations in them, Hume points out, in connection with his theory of personal identity, the ways in which such alterations may occur without affecting belief in substantial identity. Trivial alterations will pass unnoticed, as will those of magnitude so long as that is proportionate to the extent of the whole. "There is, however, another artifice, by which we may induce the imagination to advance a step farther; and that is, by producing a reference of the parts to each other, and a combination to some *common end* or purpose."[257] Thus a ship much altered by repairs would still be referred to as the same ship, in virtue of the common purpose served by the old and the new parts. In the case of "all animals and vegetables," there is "a *sympathy* of parts to their *common end*" in virtue of which the parts exist in "a mutual dependence on, and connection with, each other."[257] Where this is present, the object may "endure a total change," without belief in its substantial identity thereby being affected.

In the next stage of his explanation of the nature of our belief in bodies, Hume's position is not altogether clear. For he now tells us that though this extension of present experience by habits of causal inference "may seem to be of the same nature with our reasonings concerning causes and effects; as being derived from custom and regulated by past experience"; yet the truth is that this kind of causal inference arises "from custom in an indirect and oblique manner."[197] Accordingly, Hume goes on to point out that "as all reasoning concerning matters of fact arises only from custom, and custom can only be the effect of repeated perceptions, the extending of custom and reasoning beyond the perceptions can never be the direct and natural effect of the constant repetition and connection, but must arise from the co-operation of some other principles."[198] The first of these principles is that propensity of the imagination by which it transcends the system of the memory and the senses, "and like a galley put in motion by the oars, carries on its course without any new impulse."[198] The coherence in present perceptions is "much greater and more uniform" if it be extended to comprehend belief in their continued existence.[198] This extension of the present in imagination to include the continued existence of present effects and their causes results from that propensity of the imagination just described, "and gives us a notion of a much greater regularity among objects, than what they have when we look no farther than our senses."[198] The remaining "principles" which co-operate with habit in the connection are the constancy and coherence of perceptions.

Since Hume's view of causal inference is a theory of inference as transitive,[73, 74] it is difficult to explain why he has emphasized the transitive propensity of imagination before this only in his discussion of geometry. But, regrettable as is that neglect in analysis, Hume's general position here is inconsistent with his theory of causal inference only if we suppose that theory to be one of repetition in imagination merely. For now Hume is telling us that this extension by causal inference cannot arise from custom alone, but requires also the operation of the transitive impulse of imagination. The charge of inconsistency here would then refer to the statement that this extension by inference of the coherence in perceptions is "considerably different" from "our reasonings concerning causes and effects." For on Hume's theory of causal inference there can here be no radical difference at all.

Without wishing to gloss over such inconsistency as there may be on this point, another reading of the passage in question may nevertheless be suggested. The considerable difference here is the difference between "our reasonings concerning causes and effects; *as being derived from custom, and regulated by past experience,*"[197]* and such reasonings in their full nature which is to be at once habitual *and* transitive; not between causal inference as never more than habitual repetition, and causal inference as transitive.

That this may be Hume's intended meaning in the passage in question is perhaps confirmed by the fact that, particularly in the concluding sentences of this paragraph, he is concerned to point out that since custom is the effect of, and in its activity the cause of, "repeated perceptions," custom alone cannot extend imagination beyond

* My italics.

the compass of present experience. However, it is plain that here Hume does insist on the requirement for transitive causal inference of more than the habitual recollection of past associations.

Thus having described the "qualities" of imagination from which beliefs in continued existence arise, the respective natures of this constancy, coherence, and transitive impulse, now called "principles," are next examined in "a considerable compass of very profound reasoning." That he may establish his position here as so far stated, Hume must explain four points: first, "the *principium individuationis* or principle of identity" in things; secondly, "why the resemblance of our broken and interrupted perceptions induces us to attribute an identity to them"; thirdly, "Account for that propensity, which this illusion gives, to unite these broken appearances by a continued existence"; and finally, he must "explain that force and vivacity of conception which arises from the propensity."[199, 200]

Hume accordingly goes on to observe that the idea of an identity through time may be derived neither from any self-identical quality nor from any sort of multiplicity. For what is here to be explained is the origin of the idea of an object that remains in some sense the same during a span of time. The explanation is that throughout a succession of resembling perceptions there is maintained in imagination an idea of what in the successive perceptions is their resemblance. Hence this idea will be associated by this resemblance with the passing perceptions. As thus incessantly associated with perishing perceptions, the idea of their resemblance will be a belief in the continued existence of the resemblance in the successive perceptions. Hence "the principle of individuation is nothing but the *invariableness* and *uninterruptedness* of any object, through a supposed variation of time. . . ."[201] Were the successive perceptions varied or interrupted in their resemblance, the corresponding idea would likewise have to be altered, with which the persisting qualitative identity in the situation would disappear.

This explanation of our belief in the continued existence of what are in fact successive perceptions wherein self-identical qualities are repeated does not take account of the case where such successions are interrupted by long periods of time. And, "that I may avoid all ambiguity and confusion on this head, I shall observe, that I here account for the opinions and belief of the vulgar with regard to the existence of body; and therefore must entirely conform myself to their manner of thinking and expressing themselves."[202] This manner of thinking derives from the fact that, unlike the philosophers who distinguish between bodies and representative perceptions,[202] "the generality of mankind" makes no such distinction, but believes perceptions to be the only objects in existence. Accordingly, "I shall at first suppose that there is only a single existence, which I shall call indifferently *object* or *perception*, according as it shall seem best to suit my purpose, understanding by both of them what any common man means by a hat, or shoe, or stone, or any other impression, conveyed to him by his senses."[202] Proceeding now to his main point, Hume reminds us of the importance of resembling impressions in the workings of association. In so doing he makes statements difficult to reconcile with his theory of the self. For he now writes of an association by resemblance among "dispositions." This is hardly consistent with a theory of the self as a system of perceptions incessantly integrated by habit. The suggestion that these "dispositions" are habits in imagination, and that Hume (like Malebranche) is assuming association by resemblance among habits, rather than inadvertently assuming a substance possessed of tendencies, would be more satisfactory if, in a footnote to the next page, and in an explanation advanced as elucidating further the effects of associated "dispositions," he had not written about the "act of the mind in surveying a succession of objects."[205] Since, however, the detailed argument works out consistently with the supposition of association among habits, we may regard either the implied inconsistency with Hume's theory of the self, or the actual consistency with the supposition in question, as inadvertent, and go on to Hume's main point.

The principle of his argument here is "of great moment; and we may establish it for a general rule, that whatever ideas place the mind in the same disposition or in similar ones, are very apt to be confounded."[203] Like habits will be associated in virtue of the resemblance of their respective contents. In virtue of this resemblance, any one of the images thus associated to form the distinct but resembling habits might be substituted for any other one of them in any one of the several habits. Hence the recurrence of any such content would "place the mind" in a "disposition," or habit, the same in feeling as some other such habit, because in virtue of its resemblance with the respective contents of the two habits the image might as well be associated with the one as with the other. Hence Hume's explanation of how a succession of resembling perceptions[206] is mistaken for the continued existence of something self-identical. The absence of felt difference in the successive perceptions results in their unnoticed association with any one of several similar habits. Because the association is unnoticed, the occurrence of the succession as such is ignored. Therefore, in virtue of the habits thus involved, we habitually mistake a succession of interrupted but resembling perceptions for "only one object."[204]

This would seem to be part of Hume's meaning when, in writing of the effects in this connection of association by resemblance, he says, "The very nature and essence of relation is to connect our ideas with each other, and upon the appearance of one, to facilitate the transition to its correlative. The passage betwixt related ideas is, therefore, so smooth and easy, that it produces little alteration on the mind, and seems like the continuation of the same action; and as the continuation of the same action is an effect of the continued view of the same object, it is for this reason we attribute sameness to every succession of related objects."[204] If, for "the mind," we read here "the system" of perceptions related by the natural relation of cause and effect which Hume finds to be the true nature of the mind, we will understand "the passage betwixt ideas" to mean the passing by association from one perception to its resembling "correlative." Because this "passage" by association is so "smooth and easy" as to be unnoticed, it "produces little alteration on the mind." It is therefore in virtue of such unnoticed associations that resembling impressions are associated with resembling habits. Because of this parallel resemblance between the perceptions and the habits, any one of the perceptions will be associated indifferently with any one or all of the habits. Hence the successive association with these habits of successive but resembling perceptions will be habitually mistaken for the continued existence of a self-same perception.[204]

The importance for Hume's analysis here of the parallel resemblance between perception and habit he emphasizes in the footnote referred to above. He there observes that there are involved in the present matter "two relations, and both of them resemblances, which contribute to our mistaking the succession of our interrupted perceptions for an identical object."[205 n.] There is "the resemblance of the perceptions," and there is the resemblance of "the act of the mind in surveying a succession of resembling objects" to the act "in surveying an identical object." It is in accordance with Hume's analysis of the matter that "these resemblances we are apt to confound with each other."[205 n.] For each one of the successive perceptions will involve a habit in imagination, which will be resembling as are the perceptions. The passing by association from habit to habit being unnoticed, so also is the *succession* of perceptions. This being ignored, there can be no discriminated difference between those intrinsically resembling perceptions as successive, and *any* one of them as merely present. Hence the belief in which a resemblance repeated in successive perceptions is mistaken for the continued existence of a single perception.

This explanation of why the resemblance of interrupted perceptions[199, 200] makes us believe them to be identical throughout the interruption having been given, Hume goes on to his third question. How is it that out of the belief in continued existence the belief in independent existence arises?

Here it is the premise of the argument that "nothing is more certain from experience, than that any contradiction either to the sentiments or passions gives a sensible uneasiness, whether it proceeds from without or from within; from the opposition of external objects, or from the combat of internal principles. On the contrary, whatever strikes in with the natural propensities, and either externally forwards their satisfaction, or internally concurs with their movements, is sure to give a sensible pleasure."[205, 206] This being assumed, then in the felt opposition of belief in the continued existence of perceptions, and their absence during an interrupted existence, "the mind must be uneasy." It would seem, therefore, that either the belief must be denied, or the interruptions always pass unnoticed. Yet such beliefs are too firmly established to be annulled; and after a long interruption, recurring perceptions are sometimes unfamiliar.

Hence we are faced with two questions. We both believe in the continued existence of our perceptions, and are aware of their interrupted existence. It is therefore to be explained "how we can satisfy ourselves in supposing a perception to be absent from the mind without being annihilated."[207] Though the appearance of a perception be interrupted, belief in its continued existence is not thereby arrested, but still persists. This persistent belief in the continued existence of a perception is a denial of its intermittent annihilation and re-creation.

The second question turns on the fact that within this belief in continued existence there is implicated no claim that a perception is brought into or out of existence by the presence or absence of ourselves. "When we are absent from it, we say it still exists, but that we do not feel, we do not see it. When we are present, we say we feel, or see it."[207] Our second question, then, is how the recurrence of a perception is to be understood "without some new creation of a perception or image; and what we mean by this *seeing*, and *feeling*, and *perceiving*."[207]

The first of these two questions Hume answers in a short paragraph. The mind being "nothing but a heap or collection of different perceptions, united together by certain relations, . . ." and all perceptions, in virtue of their distinctness, being separable, "it evidently follows, that there is no absurdity in separating any particular perception from the mind; that is, in breaking off all its relations with that connected mass of perceptions, which constitute a thinking being."[207] Since what is distinguishable is separable, distinct perceptions may be separate existences, with the consequence that their annihilation is not implied by any interruption in their presence to the mind.

The same considerations indicate the answer to the first part of the second question, concerning the "new creation" of recurring perceptions. Perceptions being distinct, and therefore separable existences, they may "without absurdity" be believed to exist independently of the mind. Thus, on the ground that what is distinguishable is separable, Hume writes: "The same continued and uninterrupted Being may, therefore, be sometimes present to the mind, and sometimes absent from it, without any real or essential change in the Being itself. An interrupted appearance to the senses implies not necessarily an interruption in the existence. The supposition of the continued existence of sensible objects or perceptions involves no contradiction. We may easily indulge our inclination to that supposition."[207-8] Although the continued existence of perceptions is not demonstrable, neither is it demonstrable that to be is to be perceived.

The second part of his second question, Hume answers in short order. "If the name of *perception* renders not this separation from a mind absurd and contradictory, the name of *object*, standing for the very same thing, can never render their conjunction impossible."[207] Since, in virtue of their distinctness, perceptions are to one another wholly external, there can be no more difficulty in the "conjunction" of perceptions than in their separateness. Hence, as there is no absurdity in affirming the continued existence of perceptions no longer conjoined with that system which is the mind, so is there no difficulty in the recurrent association of perceptions within that same system. Consequently, "what we mean by this *seeing*, and *feeling*, and *perceiving*"[207] is that a perception which, on the principle that what is distinguishable is separable, may be the same "Being" that occurred before in association with the mind, is again thus conjoined with that system.

Hume's two questions are thus both answered on the same principle. The distinct being the separable, distinct perceptions are intrinsically external to, or wholly independent of, one another. This being so, there can be no absurdity in the statement that perceptions may exist independently of a mind; with the consequence that the being of a perception does not depend on its being in the relationship that defines a mind. By the same token, Hume argues,[207] it follows that there is also no difficulty in explaining the perceiving of a perception or object. For that perceptions, being external to one another, should be conjoined in association, and so be aware of themselves as such, we are as free to observe in fact as we are to assume their separate existence in which they would be aware of nothing at all beyond themselves.

The confusion in association of resembling perceptions by which a succession of perceptions is believed to be a single constant thing is thus shown to be "without absurdity." Hence, "When the exact resemblance of our perceptions makes us ascribe to them an identity, we may remove the seeming interruption by feigning a continued being, which may fill those intervals, and preserve a perfect and entire identity to our perceptions."[208] And that is how the belief in distinct (or independent) existence derives from the belief in a continued existence. Were the imagination not free to feign the continued independent existence of perceptions believed to be continuous in their existence, there would be a conflict between the belief in continued existence and the awareness of interrupted existence. That the mind is free to

believe in the independent existence of perceptions, Hume considers he has shown on the
ground that what is distinguishable is separable:
that the mind is forced to feign the independent
existence of perceptions believed to be continuous
in their existence, Hume urges on the further
ground that only in this way may felt interruptions
in the existence of such perceptions be reconciled
with the belief in their continued existence.

II

In order further to analyse the explanation of
our belief in continued and independent existence,
we must, it would seem, first ask about the nature
of what has, or, in part is, this belief. What we
can know of the mind, Hume finds, is a bundle
of perceptions. But by strands of what sort is this
bundle tied together? By the natural relations of
resemblance and causation, is the answer.[260] In
virtue of their resemblance in certain respects,
successive perceptions are in such respects felt as
indifferently the same, and hence as constant in
their succession. This felt indifference or familiar-
ity of successive perceptions is here explained by
the mechanism of recollection. On the supposition
that we could witness the operations of a mind
which "always preserves the memory of a considerable part of [its] past perceptions," it will be

plain, Hume thinks, that nothing "could more contribute to the bestowing a relation on this succession amidst all its variations" than this constant recollection.[260] "For what is the memory but a faculty, by which we raise up the images of past perceptions? And as an image necessarily resembles its object, must not the frequent placing of these resembling perceptions in the chain of thought convey the imagination more easily from one link to another, and make the whole seem like the continuance of one object?"[260, 261] This assumes the incessant working of habits, of which the contents, constantly recollected, are incessantly associated within present perceptions. The association here is association by resemblance. It is in virtue of this incessant association of recollections with impressions that the habit of feeling these elements of perceptions as indifferent or constantly familiar is engendered.

Yet the felt continuity of experience involves more than the repetition in imagination of images qualitatively identical with those produced by unknown causes. For there are also the irregularities in experience to be accounted for. Up to this point, Hume's explanation of the felt continuity of successive perceptions runs parallel to that part of his explanation of belief in the continued existence of bodies which relies on a facility for mistaking successive resemblances for single identities. And so much as this, here, means only that repeated or recollected imagery is in an incessant and unnoticed association within present perceptions. Because no prominent differences are felt, and because the association itself of these resembling recollections within present perceptions is unnoticed, within such experience there is felt not a succession, but a constant continuity in mnemonic and sensory imagery. The felt continuity of personal identity being thus accounted for, it remains to explain how the felt variety and conflict within our experience is to be accounted for in relation to this felt continuity.

The burden of this explanation is borne by the second of the two strands by which successive perceptions are tied into a bundle. "As to *causation*; we may observe, that the true idea of the human mind is to consider it as a system of different perceptions or different existences, which are linked together by the relation of cause and effect, and mutually produce, destroy, influence, and modify each other."[261] The felt activity of the natural relation of cause and effect is the feeling of perceptions whose succession is felt in anticipation either as necessary, probable, or merely possible.

In all those cases of established habits of causal inference which are in no conflict within or among themselves, the activity would be felt as necessary and its issue as a proof. It is in such cases as these, wherein the perception anticipated as cause or effect is evoked (as it were) automatically, that perceptions would "mutually produce each other."

Again, in all cases of conflicts between habits of causal inference, there then would be either the outright elimination of the weaker association by the stronger, or the development of the felt probabilities of chance and cause. The elimination of weaker associations would be felt as the exclusion of an impossibility; whereas the entertaining of an image more or less free from associations would be felt as a possibility, which might be so gratuitous as to be a mere fancy or chance. In the course of the elimination of weaker associations, and the formation of felt probabilities, causal associations would "influence and modify each other" in point of force and vivacity.

That such variety in belief may be felt as existing within a single system, the continuity of that system must be realized and felt constantly in the variety of beliefs. How this can be is explained by the fact that, on Hume's theory, association by resemblance is a condition at once of the felt constancy of the self, and of the existence of the natural relation of cause and effect existing as proofs and probabilities. Thus the association by resemblance which allows for the felt continuity is also the association of constant conjuncts which, in the case of "perfect" habits, issues in a continuity of the present with the anticipated felt so strongly as to feel inevitable or necessary. Felt probabilities, we have seen, are causal inferences issuing from conflicts among habits which, though in conflict among themselves, are in themselves formed through association by resemblance. This mode of association is thus the active principle both of the continuity of the self and of the formation of the natural relation of cause and effect, itself the source of proofs and probabilities in all their variety. The principle of the continuity of the mind is therefore internal to and operative in the habits of causal inference which, together with perceptions of bodies, ideas general in their reference, and fancies, constitute the diverse perceptions of the understanding.

As thus conceived of, how is a mind to be distinguished from a body? In view of Hume's flat statement at the outset of his *Scepticism with regard to the Senses*, that the existence of body is to be taken for granted throughout all our reasonings, and that he is concerned only to ask about what causes induce us to believe in the existence of matter, the answer to our question may seem to be a foregone conclusion. Bodies are the unknowable objects of our beliefs in their continued, independent existence; and, as such, are separate from the minds possessing those beliefs.

To this answer one objection immediately suggests itself. Since these bodies would be unknowable, how could they be believable? Any belief must have content: it must be belief in a somewhat. Yet, in this case, what could be the content? Surely not anything known to belong to bodies, *ex hypothesi* unknowable. The contents must then be what is believed to be the attributes of body. But can this alternative be open to us on Hume's theory of belief in matter? On that theory the contents of the belief in question are of course impressions and ideas in association. And the definition of belief as a lively idea associated with a present impression would seem to exclude any notion of a reference transcending the nature of belief itself. Yet without this transcendence, how can belief in bodies be felt as the reference of the present perception to an unknowable reality lying beyond the perception itself?

The answer to this question may seem to be obvious: the tendency to feign an independent existence is this reference. The referent of the reference is unknown, but the reference itself is the habit that is our constant belief in an external world.

Yet to this interpretation of the matter in

question there are several objections to be made. Writing of his sceptical analysis of our belief in matter, and of his account of the causes of that belief, Hume says: "The natural consequence of this reasoning should be, that our perceptions have no more a continued than an independent existence; and indeed philosophers have so far run into this opinion that they change their system, and distinguish (as we shall do for the future) betwixt perceptions and objects, of which the former are supposed to be interrupted, and perishing, and different at every different return; the latter to be uninterrupted, and to preserve a continued existence and identity."[211] In short, the distinction between primary and secondary qualities is made by philosophers in order that belief in permanence may be reconciled with apparent change. "But however philosophical this new system may be esteemed, I assert that it is only a palliative remedy, and that it contains all the difficulties of the vulgar system, with some others, that are peculiar to itself."[211] And the remainder of *Scepticism with regard to the Senses* is given over to showing that "this opinion of the double existence" of perceptions and objects is neither rational nor anything invented by the imagination; and that its entire plausibility derives from the "common hypothesis" on which all objects are perceptions.

Belief in Substance

The philosophical theory of an order of objects independent of perceptions cannot be rational, for we can transcend present experience only by the natural relation of cause and effect. This relation, we have noticed, cannot exist between perceptions and what *ex hypothesi* lies beyond all experience. The suggestion that the belief in question may be an invention of the imagination alone and unaided by association and habit, Hume does not find at all persuasive. But if it can be explained to Hume how, from distinct and interrupted perceptions, the imagination "directly and immediately proceeds to the belief of another existence, resembling these perceptions in their nature, but yet continued, and uninterrupted, and identical,"[213] he will then retract his assertion that imagination without custom is not the origin of the belief in independent existence. Therefore, since the philosophical theory of representative perception originates neither in reason nor in mere imagination, that theory "*acquires all its influence on the imagination from the vulgar one*."[213] In order that we may eliminate the felt conflict between our belief in continued existence and our awareness of the interrupted existence of our perceptions, we habitually feign not only a continued but also an independent existence. This continued and independent existence is for the vulgar simply that of the perceptions themselves.

Hence, when Hume is concerned with "the vulgar hypothesis," he is at pains to explain the respects in which it fits what *may* be the facts of the case.

Philosophers, finding it difficult to understand how perceptions can be at once mind-dependent and independent existences, seek to improve on the vulgar assumption with the theory that only some qualities are in fact independent and constant realities. Yet this learned opinion, being the invention neither of causal inference nor of mere imagination, can derive its persuasive force only from the vulgar opinion in the matter. That it should do so is no more than natural. In the vulgar opinion, what appears to be a thing is assumed to have an independent existence. The belief in independent existence is thus habitual and natural. The philosophical theory about primary and secondary qualities seeks to clarify this assumption by distinguishing qualities alleged to be independent in their existence from those which are mere perceptions. Actually, however, the natural belief in independent existence derives not from this distinction in theory, but from the everyday habits in imagination whose origin and constitution Hume has sought to analyse.

In reply to the objection that, in his theory about space, Hume makes no attempt to explain the nature of empty space, he writes: "I answer this objection by pleading guilty, and by confessing that my intention never was to penetrate into the nature of bodies, or explain the secret causes of their operations. For besides that this belongs not to my present purpose, I am afraid that such an enterprise is beyond the reach of human understanding, and we can never pretend to know body otherwise than by those external properties, which discover themselves to the senses."[64] These statements, together with the declaration made at the outset of his sceptical analysis of our uncritical assumption of an external world, would seem to make it plain that Hume is assuming a domain of matter whose existence transcends experience. For this assumption, the philosophical theory of representative perception and that on which primary and secondary qualities are distinguished afford no justification. It can be demonstrated neither by sense-perception nor by reason. Yet the natural belief in the continued and independent existence of perceived things remains to be explained by the discovery of its causes. Hence, Hume is concerned to make it plain that although the vulgar belief in perceptions as continued and independent existences is denied by the philosophical, nevertheless that belief is incompatible neither with the nature of perceptions nor with that of the mind.

In so far as bodies can be known in sense-experience, they will consist of "those external properties, which discover themselves to the senses."[64] Perceived bodies will be the perceptions that would be properly called bodies on the vulgar hypothesis. Our main question may thus appear to admit of no satisfactory answer. Perceived bodies and minds both being perceptions, how can they be distinguished? The difficulty here is not lessened by the fact that Hume's explanation of belief in continued existence is largely alike for both bodies and minds. In both cases it is the "gross illusion . . . that our resembling perceptions are numerically the same"[217] by which that belief is explained. Yet if this sharpens the difficulty it also narrows the question at issue. For we have only to enquire whether or not Hume's explanation of the belief in independent existence is different from his theory of the self as a system of perceptions.

The perceptions which the uncritical call bodies are those that are constant and coherent in their occurrence. This constancy and coherence is peculiar to these perceptions alone. Association by resemblance is common both to the belief in the *continued existence* of such perceptions as are called bodies and to the felt *continuity* in the succession of perceptions within the causal system that is the self. The italics may serve to bring out the point that in the one case perceptions are believed to continue in existence when unrelated with a mind, whereas in the other there is no question of the continued existence of a perception, but only of the continuous, or uninterrupted, succession of perceptions. To explain this continuity, a soul or spiritual substance in which these perceptions inhere is uncritically assumed. But no perceptions not exhibiting the constancy and coherence of perceived things are believed to continue in existence apart from the mind. Therefore, the perceptions not believed to have a continued existence will not be believed to have an independent existence. Such perceptions related by the natural relation of cause and effect will constitute the mind.

The impressions and ideas associated to form perceptions of perceived things will be such as are constant in their resemblance and coherent in their differences. Their constancy and coherence differentiate the elements of such perceptions from the impressions and ideas associated to constitute the perceptions of the mind. This indicates what is the fundamental difference between "external" and "internal" perceptions. The elements of the former are associated by resemblance. It is also in virtue of such association that complex ideas recollected are felt as continuous with perceptions present. Yet whereas the habits in imagination engendered by the constant repetition of, and the coherent alteration in, perceived things are sensory-mnemonic in content, the habits which constitute what of the self does persist through the actual succession of its perceptions are the habits of causal inference. Association by resemblance is integral to both of these systems of habits. Yet habits of causal inference involve a factor not present in the system of the memory and the senses, and not reducible to the repetition of images in association. This factor, we have noticed, is the transitive impulse of imagination, by which we people the world of ourselves.

The defining difference between objective and subjective perceptions thus is that in their constitution the former are sensory-mnemonic, whereas the latter are at once mnemonic and transitive. Within a belief in the continued and independent existence of a perception, all is the association of constant and coherent content by resemblance. That is why, within my belief in the continued and independent existence of what I call my table, there is no feeling of that perception as expecting anything beyond itself. Thus, within this perception of my table, there is no expectation of the perceptions which would precede its being spotted with ink.

The perceptions of which a mind at any moment will consist being both mnemonic and expectant, they are felt to be at once continuous with those past, and to be expecting with a felt necessity or (as the case may be) probability a future resembling the past. Perceptions uncritically called bodies thus will naturally appear as self-contained and without reference beyond themselves. The perceptions which, at any one moment, are related by the natural relation of cause and effect will feel themselves not as self-contained, but as expectant.

Whenever what coherently changes in perceptions is not continuously apparent within the perceptions themselves, the causes and effects required for the coherence thus lacking will be inferred in imagination by the natural relation of cause and effect. The imagination will thus extend the realities of the system of the memory and the senses beyond their own presented scope. In so doing, the self transcends not its own transitive beliefs, but only those perceptions which anticipate nothing beyond their own existence.

The question "of the immateriality of the soul"[232] is thus not to be decided by "the curious reasoners concerning the material or immaterial substances, in which they suppose perceptions to inhere."[232] For, having no impression either of substance or of inherence, these reasoners can find nothing in experience corresponding to their views. The Cartesian definition of a substance, moreover, is of no avail in the matter. For if "a substance is *something which may exist by itself*," then perceptions, since they are separable, are substances.[233]

Hence, neither in experience nor in the Cartesian definition is any idea of substance as different from perception to be found: "which seems to me a sufficient reason for abandoning utterly that dispute concerning the materiality and immateriality of the soul, and makes me absolutely condemn even the question itself."[234] Hume nevertheless goes on to consider an argument for the immateriality of the soul, which he finds "remarkable." The argument is that matter, being divisible, cannot co-exist with thought, which is indivisible. This argument, Hume finds, is really concerned not with the substance of the soul, but rather with the question of its "local conjunction" with matter. Consequently, Hume will examine a "curious question"; viz. what "objects" are capable of local conjunction; an examination which "may lead us to some discoveries of considerable moment."[235]

This curious question may be exhaustively analysed, Hume thinks, into three alternatives. On the first of these, some "objects" have *no* place. On the second, all objects have some position or other; although, in some cases, this position may consist in occupying a "mathematical point." On the third, some objects, although unextended, are nevertheless wholly present in what is extended. Since only what is coloured, tangible, and figured is properly speaking extended, the first of these alternatives is true, and the second and third are false. Tastes, odours, sounds, being neither coloured nor tangible nor figured, are not extended. "A moral reflection cannot be placed on the right or on the left hand of a passion, nor can a smell or sound be either of a circular or a square figure."[236] The relish of an olive seems to permeate the olive as a whole, and a sound will seem to have a position in space. But this happens because, in imagination, we add a spatial position to the causal and temporal union in perception of the taste and the olive.

It is thus plain that the materialist is in part mistaken. There are unextended perceptions which exist nowhere.[235] If matter be identified with the extended, this means that some perceptions are "immaterial." Yet the materialist is also in the right; for there are extended perceptions. "That table, which just now appears to me, is only a perception, and all its qualities are qualities of a perception. Now the most obvious of all its qualities is extension."[239] And Hume goes on to describe this "most obvious quality" as having parts, figure, and position. Thus, "the free-thinker may now triumph in his turn";[240] for how is a simple, immaterial substance to be viewed as "incorporated" with extended perceptions? To the questions to which this gives rise it is impossible to give any answer that would be less than absurd.[240]

Yet, though Hume has "condemned" as "utterly unintelligible" all questions concerning the substance of the soul, he will take this occasion further to show the inanity of the entire issue. This he does by arguing at length that those immaterialists who have attempted to refute Spinoza have done so by reasonings which, properly understood, refute their own immaterialism. On the "hideous hypothesis" of Spinoza all things are modifications of a single, simple substance.[240] On the hypothesis of the theologians,* things "also are modifications, and modifications of one simple, uncompounded, and indivisible substance."[242] Yet our perceptions of the sun, moon, and stars remain on either hypothesis unchanged either in fact or in theory. Why, then, in attributing our perceptions to the substance of Spinoza should there be difficulties not present in their being attributed to the no less simple and indivisible substance of the theologians? The answer, Hume finds, is that both hypotheses have "the same fault of being unintelligible, and

* See, for example, *Réfutation des Erreurs de Benoit de Spinoza*, par M. de Fénelon, le P. Lamy, et M. le Comte de Boullainvilliers. Avec *La Vie de Spinoza*, par M. Jean Colerus. Brussels, 1731.

that as far as we can understand them, they are
so much alike, that it is impossible to discover
any absurdity in one which is not common to
both of them."[243] Even though these considerations are "beyond doubt and contradiction,"
Hume pursues the point, as we shall not, to show
the absurdities in his understanding of Spinoza's
hypothesis to be common to his conception of
that of the theologians.

There remains, however, an argument for
immaterialism, which Hume finds at once more
intelligible and more important than the views on
that subject he has so far examined. Matter and
motion, it is urged, can cause only matter and
motion.[246] Despite the fact that this argument for
immaterialism is commonly regarded as irrefra-
gable, nothing is easier than to refute it.[247] For
a priori, anything may be the cause of anything.
Even with respect to motions, our opinion that
they are causes and effects is a belief, the contradictory of which is imaginable. Hence, "since
every one may perceive that the different dispositions of his body change his thoughts and
sentiments," "there seems only this dilemma left
us in the present case; either to assert, that
nothing can be the cause of another, but where
the mind can perceive the connection in its idea
of the objects: Or to maintain, that all objects,
which we find constantly conjoined, are upon that

account to be regarded as causes and effects."[248] Since no logical necessity obtaining between ideas is to be found, to adopt the first alternative would be to deny all meaning to the terms cause and effect. As for the contention of Malebranche that we perceive a necessary connection between the omnipotence of the Creator and all that happens, this amounts to the assertion "that a being, whose volition is connected with every effect, is connected with every effect."[249] Since this is an "identical proposition" it in no way elucidates the nature of the alleged connection.

The second alternative remains. Those perceptions which are constantly and habitually expected as such are causes and effects. Evidently, then, perceptions habitually called bodies may be said to cause perceptions in a mind. In his "final" decision upon the materialist and immaterialist theories of the soul, Hume again roundly declares the entire question of the substance of the soul to be "absolutely unintelligible." The materialist, however, has the advantage over his adversary. For although perceptions which are not extended exist, it is also quite plain that, in the one sense in which the term cause can have meaning, bodies may be said to cause ideas.

The basic reason why the dualism of the Cartesians and the monistic theories of Spinoza and the theologians are alike in being unintelli-

gible is that the one like the others makes asser-
tions about a reality that would lie beyond the
scope of perception. But any such reality can only
lie beyond our ken. Hume unintentionally emphasizes the inanity of his own assumption of a
transcendental domain of matter when he writes:
"Let us fix our attention out of ourselves as much
as possible: Let us chase our imagination to the
heavens, or to the utmost limits of the universe;
we never really advance a step beyond ourselves,
nor can conceive any kind of existence, but
those perceptions which have appeared in that
narrow compass. This is the universe of the
imagination, nor have we any idea but what is
there produced."[67, 68] The distinction between
bodies and minds, commonly made in discourse,
is thus to be explained within the limits of the
imagination. The referent of the term body may
be any perception wherein there is constant
repetition and coherent, if any, variation. Hence
the difference between perceived bodies and minds
is neither to be explained by the dualism of the
Cartesians, nor to be denied on the monistic
doctrines of Spinoza and the theologians; it is
rather to be made out by noticing that perceived
bodies are mnemonic-sensory systems, whereas
minds are systems within which alone the natural
relation of cause and effect exists and operates.

Mr. Laird finds that "Hume's account of the

self did not attempt to discriminate between what was 'internal' (cf. 319) and what was apparently 'external' in the heap of perceptions."* It is to be regretted that in his account of personal identity Hume does not bring out the differences which, on his theories, are to be found between perceived bodies and minds. It would be too much to suggest, however, that on the basis of those theories Hume makes out no difference at all between such perceptions as are believed by the vulgar to be distinct existences, and therefore external, and such perceptions as do not believe themselves to constitute things. Yet Mr. Laird more than suggests this when he writes, "Again, since 'the system of the memory and senses,' according to Hume 'peopled the world,' that is to say, *constituted* the world *quoad nos* (than which we could conceive no other world), it seems clear that the mental 'heap' must differ in some empirical way from the 'world' itself."†

For his quotations here, Mr. Laird gives no reference. Presumably, however, the text intended is that[108] wherein the system which is "the object of the memory and the senses" is distinguished from that which is the object of "the judgment." Yet, according to Hume, it is the second of these two systems, not the first, which peoples the

* John Laird, *Hume's Philosophy of Human Nature*, p. 174.
† Ibid.

world. This it does, not in constituting the world of perceived bodies, but in making us "acquainted with such existences, as by their removal in time and place, lie beyond the reach of the senses and memory."[108] This second system of perceptions, related by the natural relation of cause and effect, is the mind. In virtue of the operations of that relation, the mind peoples the world of its imagination with ideas of perceptions anticipated as inevitable or probable. Although Hume does not compare perceived bodies and minds (beyond actually contrasting the two systems to which Mr. Laird refers), they would appear to be definitely different in the empirical way in which the natural relation of resemblance differs from that of cause and effect.

A further difficulty of Mr. Laird's also may be noticed. For Hume, " 'causes' were only associative expectations. Therefore the mental 'heap' could not really be connected *by causation* in the same objective sense as the constituents might *resemble* one another."* Yet, that perceptions are thus connected by causation is the only intelligible construction Mr. Laird can put on Hume's definition of the true idea of the mind.

The sense for Hume in which perceptions are resembling merely, is the sense in which resemblance is a philosophical relation. Likewise, the

* John Laird, *Hume's Philosophy of Human Nature*, p. 174.

sense in which perceptions are associated by resemblance is the sense in which that term designates a natural relation. That neither of these is Mr. Laird's objective sense in which perceptions might be resembling is perhaps plain. Yet, in the sense in which Hume uses the term in question to designate a connection, resemblance is a natural relation, as is also causation. That within and between the perceptions of the mind there is association by causation means that within and between perceptions the natural relation of cause and effect exists. The sense, then, in which perceptions are connected by causation is the same as that in which they are connected by resemblance. For in the sense in which the two terms in question refer to connections, they both denote natural relations. And since the workings of "perfect" cases of the habit of causal inference, *felt* as inevitable, afford the impression of reflection from which the idea of necessity is derived, the conclusion that this necessity exists in the mind, not in perceived bodies, is no more than consistent with the existence of causation as the defining relation of the perceptions of the mind. Taking Hume at his word, then, on the meaning of resemblance as designating either or both a philosophical and a natural relation, perceptions may be related as well by the natural relation of causation as by that of resemblance.

Belief in Substance

That throughout the *Treatise*, Hume assumes the reality of effective causation (as opposed to the philosophical relation of cause and effect), is a proposition hardly needing defence, although the extent of its bearing does require consideration. References to the natural relations as "giving rise to," "producing," and plain "causing" perceptions are plentiful. There are also the "unknown causes" from which impressions arise. Had Hume asserted that we have no idea of causation, the contradiction in theory would have been flagrant. In fact, Hume agrees with "the Cartesians" that of causation as a relation between things, defined in terms of logical necessity, we have no idea. He turns his own development of their critique of efficient causation as so defined against their own conclusion that we do see a necessary connection between the omnipotence of God and the happenings in nature. Our idea of causation, Hume finds, is an idea of habitual conjunction *felt* to be necessary. Since this felt necessity is an impression or determination, of "perfect" habits of association, our idea of the effective force of causation is our idea of the "gentle force." There is, it would seem, no reason for supposing that Hume thought of association as anything other than an effective agency. The causal efficacy of association not being defined as a logically necessary connection (the contradictory of which would be in every case inconceivable), there is no contradiction in denying causation as defined by Malebranche, and in asserting causation as a natural relation consisting of constant conjunctions effectively connected by the gentle force. Within things, the philosophical relation of cause and effect, which is the natural relation of causation considered with respect to its constantly conjoined content alone, is all Hume can find. But within the mind there is the impression of reflection of what—both for "the Cartesians" and for Hume—is the defining characteristic of causation, i.e. necessity. This necessity, however, is not that of "the Cartesians," but rather is the felt force of the workings of habits of expectation. Within and between perceived bodies, the philosophical relation of cause and effect is all of the natural relation of causation that is to be found. Necessity is found to exist not in perceived bodies, but in the mind. This felt necessity being the defining characteristic of causation, Hume is wholly consistent both with his theory about the nature of that relation, and his denial of its alleged logical necessity, in finding that the natural relation of causation is the defining connection within and between the perceptions of the mind. Since Hume not only does not deny, but explains, that the workings of this natural relation in perceptions, whether felt as proofs, probabilities, chances, or possibilities, do give rise to, produce, and eliminate perceptions, there would seem to be no reason why (on Hume's own theory) perceptions "could not really be connected by *causation*."

Here it may be objected that if in virtue of its gentle force the relation of causation is effectively causal, then by the same token the natural relation of resemblance is effectively causal also. On at least two counts, this would seem to be Hume's theory. (1) Since both relations are forms of association, both are ways in which the gentle force acts. (2) Both are referred to as producing ideas and perceptions. The question then would be, why, if both relations are in effect causal, only one of them is so designated by Hume. To this the answer is perhaps not far to seek. As distinguished from resemblance, the nature of the natural relation of causation is to be expectant; its defining characteristic is the felt necessity of the expected. Within associations by resemblance no expectancy is felt. Thus perceptions called bodies are not felt as expecting anything beyond themselves. A perception designated at once "body" *and* "cause" would be a perception whose actual contents have been constantly conjoined with other images. These other images would be present in imagination and felt as *effects expected* in perceptions to come. Thus, though the two natural relations are alike in being "forces," they are differentiated by the absence from the one and the presence in the other of expectation. Since the impression of this expectancy felt as necessary is the origin of our idea of necessity; itself the defining characteristic of cause and effect; only cases of association wherein expectation is involved are (by definition) properly called cases of causation.

That Hume also believed in the existence of "unknown causes" would seem to be clear. This belief is at least consistent with his own positive theory of causal inference, which does not imply that what we cannot find may not exist. Yet, at best, Hume's right to this belief in "unknown causes" would be difficult to justify. In the first place, what could be the content of such a belief? Only our perceptions themselves, it would seem; and they certainly are not unknown. In the second place, these causes, as unknown, would have to be of a nature quite different from that of association. That being so, Hume's theory of causation and causal inference plainly cannot claim to be adequate to at least one of his own assumptions. Yet it is difficult to see how Hume could abandon his assumption of these unknown causes. For, as T. H. Green has so amply made plain, without that assumption Hume's statement of his first principle would be less than plausible. His critical analysis of the causal relation, however, does not depend on his theory of impressions and ideas. Therefore, that his assumption of unknown causes of impressions may be required for the effective statement of that theory, does not imply that assumption to be required by the critical analysis itself.

CHAPTER V

Knowledge and Belief

"By knowledge," Hume says, "I mean the assurance arising from the comparison of ideas."[124] But not, he explains, the assurance which arises from the comparison of no matter what ideas. For of the seven philosophical relations, only four yield knowledge; and it is characteristic of these four relations that they "depend entirely on the ideas, which we compare together."[69] It is thus Hume's view that resemblance, degrees of quality, contrariety, and proportions in quantity and number are relations which "depend entirely" on their terms.[70]

Since in Hume's view the resemblance of any two qualities is the qualitative identity of the qualities themselves, it is plain that the substitution of different qualities would be *ipso facto* the substitution of a different resemblance or qualitative identity. "It is the same case with all the degrees in any quality. They are all resembling, and yet the quality, in any individual, is not distinct from the degree."[637] In the case of the range of a single hue deepening in saturation, for example, the *degree* of saturation is not distinguishable from the *saturation* discriminated. Like the philosophical relation of resemblance, that of degrees in quality is exhausted in its terms.

The philosophical relation of contrariety involves difficulties which need not be mentioned again. But as a relation which depends entirely on its terms, contrariety is one of the three philosophical relations which "are discoverable at first sight, and fall more properly under the province of intuition than demonstration."[70] Although difficulty may sometimes be felt in discriminating nuances of difference in degrees of quality, whenever the difference is considerable its discrimination will be a matter of direct inspection. But in the case of contrariety "no one can once doubt but existence and non-existence destroy each other, and are perfectly incompatible and contrary."[70] And most cases of resemblance will be apparent at once; "a second examination" being seldom required.

Because comparisons in point of resemblance, degrees of quality, and contrariety are intuitive, all such comparisons will be unmediated by doubt. But the absolute assurance arising from intuitive comparison does not exhaust the meaning of the term "knowledge" for Hume. In any case of knowledge the contradictory will be inconceivable.* Since cases of resemblance and degree

* "Such an inference would amount to knowledge, and would imply the absolute contradiction and impossibility of conceiving any thing different," p. 87.

of quality are for Hume cases of qualitative identity, it is plainly inconceivable that any case of such identity should be both itself and not itself. Knowledge is thus at once unmediated by doubt and formally certified.

In all cases of proportions of quantity or number, "where the difference is very great and remarkable," we may "proceed after the same manner" of direct comparison, and "at one view observe a superiority or inferiority betwixt any numbers or figures."[70] But where the matter at hand requires more than the direct comparison of simple proportions, we must "proceed in a more *artificial* manner";[70] viz. that of inference. Thus, because proportions in quantity and number are in fact not reducible to philosophical relations, or relations of comparison in point of identity merely, Hume is obliged to distinguish "the manner" of their treatment from that of genuine philosophical relations.

Because the demonstrations of geometry employ the absurdity of infinite divisibility, that art "fails of evidence in this single point, while all its other reasonings command our fullest assent and approbation."[52] There is thus the difficulty of explaining how it is that geometry can be an art so admirable and yet based on an absurd conception of extension.[52] Accordingly, Hume seeks to find a foundation for geometry in sense-experience. It is "evident," he finds, that the definitions given of surface, line, and point are "perfectly unintelligible upon any other supposition than that of the composition of extension by indivisible points or atoms."[42] For otherwise nothing corresponding to the definition of a point could exist.

As for the objection that the points are ideal and in no sense existential, nothing "more absurd and contradictory" can be imagined.[42, 43] The reason why the absurdity here is egregious is that the idea of a point either "implies the possibility of existence" or it is not an idea at all.[43] The alternative of denying the idea of a point is that elected by the authors of *L'Art de penser*. The length, breadth, and depth of a point is inseparable from it, both in fact and in our minds; but this does not prevent their abstraction by a distinction of reason.[43] This fails, however, to meet the requirements of the case. For were the ideas of surfaces, lines, and points infinitely divisible, there could be no "terminations," with the consequence that no distinctions whatever could be made.[43, 44]

It is thus evident that the demonstrations of geometry, because they employ the absurdity of infinite divisibility, contradict the principle of its proper definitions, viz. that extension consists of indivisible points. Since on Hume's theory of the nature of extension these points are sensible, the definitions of geometry must be experiential. All pretensions to absolute accuracy in definition, therefore, must be given up.

The art of geometry "takes the dimensions and proportions of figures justly; but roughly, and with some liberty. Its errors are never considerable; nor would it err at all, did it not aspire to such an absolute perfection."[45] Though there be "few or no mathematicians" who accept the view of points as indivisible, it is on that view alone that the meaning of equality, and of proportion in quantity, can be rightly explained. Two lines are equal when in both the number of points is equal; and as the proportion of constituent points varies, the proportions of lines and surfaces thus constituted vary likewise. This explanation, though plainly correct, is no less obviously useless. For it is beyond our capacities ever to count the points of which a given line consists.[45] Nor is this fact to be avoided by those who (like Isaac Barrow, to whose *Mathematical Lectures* Hume here refers) claim equality to be definable by "congruity," or superposition. "In order to judge of this definition let us consider, that since equality is a relation, it is not, strictly speaking, a property in the figures themselves, but arises merely from the comparison which the mind makes between them."[46] Since "equality" is not a property of equal quantities, but the name of all comparisons in point of an identity in quantity, the definition of that term will not be the definition of the name of a property. Congruity, as the equivalent of equality, is hence a philosophical relation, viz. that of comparison in point of "the contact" of parts.[46] This comparison could be known to be accurate only if before the fact of comparison the parts of the one figure were known to be identical with those of the other. Therefore congruity as a definition of equality also is useless.

The true foundations of geometry being what appears in sense perception and imagination, on a proper view of that art, its definitions would be made to fit what is found, rather than any artificial and absurd standard of the Cartesian reason. "As the ultimate standard of these figures is derived from nothing but the senses and imagination, it is absurd to talk of any perfection beyond what these faculties can judge of; since the true perfection of any thing consists in its conformity to its standard."[51] Accordingly, Hume finds no absurdity in asserting of two lines which approach each other at the rate of an inch in twenty leagues, "that upon their contact they become one."[51] What appears, must be as it so is; the theories of the geometers notwithstanding.

The definitions of geometry being less than exact under any absolute, non-experiential standard, it is only in algebra and arithmetic that demonstration may become at all intricate, while maintaining "a perfect exactness and certainty."[71] Hume does not explore the implications of his acceptance of algebra and arithmetic as valid. He simply holds that we do have a precise standard of equality and proportion in numbers, viz. the idea of unity. But of what this idea is or could be a copy, he does not say.

Although in his statements about arithmetic and algebra Hume says that we can determine the equality and proportion of units "without any possibility of error,"[71] in the section devoted to *Scepticism with regard to reason* this is qualified. The "rules" of the demonstrative sciences "are certain and infallible,"[180] but our applications of them are notoriously fallible.

No mathematician, whatever his competence, neglects to check his proofs.[180] Merchants devise systems of accounting as a protection against the fallibility of their faculties. Reason is "a kind of cause, of which truth is the natural effect";[180] but an effect which may be prevented by the "irruption" of contrary causes. Because of the effects of conflicts among habits of inference, no demonstration is implicitly to be trusted, but is rather to be checked. That check in its turn must be tested, and so on until finally we "enlarge our view to comprehend a kind of history of all the instances wherein our understanding has deceived us, compared with those wherein its testimony was just and true."[180] For these reasons no one can maintain that in "a long numeration" our assurance ever exceeds that of felt probability.[181] Hence Hume flatly concludes that "all knowledge resolves itself into probability, and becomes at last of the same nature with that evidence, which we employ in common life. . . ."[181]

Since mathematical demonstration cannot be reduced to the operations of direct comparison which for Hume constitute knowledge, his only choice within the limits of his epistemology is to regard such demonstration as no more than probable. It is not plain, however, that his argument here applies to knowledge, in either of the two senses which together constitute the meaning of the term for him. For in the sense in which knowledge is the assurance arising from the direct comparison of ideas, knowledge is the finding of qualitative identities. Although the qualitative identity thus found may be mistakenly expressed in discourse, it nevertheless is found, and as such cannot be mistaken.

The sense in which knowledge is an intuited comparison of which the contradictory is inconceivable also is unaffected by his scepticism regarding *a priori* demonstration. But any case wherein a final comparison is arrived at through a succession of comparisons, each one of which is carried over by recollection, will be open to doubt. For the accuracy of the recollection at any one or at all points in the succession may properly be questioned. Although any inference of which the contradictory is inconceivable will be true, whether in a given case the requirements of this criterion have been met, again may be doubted. Hume's scepticism regarding reason thus is relevant neither to knowledge as intuitive comparison nor to the validity of the criterion of apagogic demonstration, but rather to the knowledge arrived at by a chain of comparisons or by the application of that criterion.

Because our faculties are fallible even the demonstrations of mathematics are to be doubted. This doubt in no case reaches a bed rock of certainty, but, on the contrary, finally annuls all felt certainty whatever. Here the validity of the "precise standards" and "the certain and infallible rules" of the demonstrative sciences (as opposed to the "art" of geometry) is not in question. It is rather the accuracy of the use of these standards and rules in the operations of habits in imagination that must be doubted by the scientist of human nature. The standards and rules of demonstration are thus tacitly distinguished from the habits of inference in and through which they are used.

In a lengthy footnote Hume examines a distinction which, although called "vulgar" by him, was sufficiently philosophical to have been made in Hume's own terms by Malebranche.* The distinction between conception as "the simple survey of one or more ideas," judgment as "the separating or uniting of different ideas," and reasoning as judgment mediated by further ideas, is "faulty in very considerable articles."[96 n.] Since "existence" is not a qualifying predicate, "God exists" is not a judgment. As for reasoning, whenever we infer a cause directly from its effect we reason, and yet we employ no more than two ideas. Hence, taking these acts of the understanding "in a proper light," we see that "they all resolve themselves into the first"; viz. conception.

Though for very different reasons, this had been the conclusion which Malebranche, too, wished to have accepted. Yet however adequate to comparisons in point of resemblance and degree of quality this notion of conception may be, it alone is plainly not adequate to any case of demonstration. In the "simple survey" of a case of resemblance there will be intuitive

* *Recherche*, Edn. Bouillier, Vol. I, pp. 27, 28.

certainty; but in all complicated matters of arithmetic, algebra, and geometry we go beyond the scope of this simple survey, and have not intuitive, but demonstrative, certainty. It is thus inevitable that the operations of demonstration should be treated by Hume not as acts of comparison merely, but as the operations of habits of inference. For between the two extremes there is for him no mean. The standard and the rules of the demonstrative sciences are valid irrespective of their use; but as their use is not exhausted in the act of comparing qualitative identities, the assurance of demonstration must be "reduced" to that of felt probability.

This opens the way to the scepticism of "that fantastic sect" which insists on a *total* scepticism."[183] "In every judgment, which we can form concerning probability, as well as concerning knowledge, we ought always to correct the first judgment, derived from the nature of the object, by another judgment, derived from the nature of the understanding."[181, 182] For as a little reflection has sufficed to show that demonstration cannot exceed probability, so a little reflection on the nature of the understanding as a system of habits will suffice to remind us that felt probabilities are sentient, not rational. Therefore, "having thus found in every probability, beside the original uncertainty inherent in the subject, a new uncertainty derived from the weakness of that faculty, which judges, and having adjusted these two together, we are obliged by our reason to add a new doubt derived from the possibility of error in the estimation we make of the truth and fidelity of our faculties."[182] Thus we are obliged to doubt not only the probability of our judgments, but our very powers of judgment themselves. There is, then, no limit to which we ought to restrict our doubts. For if we doubt the competence of our faculties, the validity of that very critical judgment must be doubted, "and so on *ad infinitum*, till at last there remains nothing of the original probability. . . ."[182] Hume assumes that in each judgment about the judgment, and so on, the same allowance for error must be made; an assumption which Mr. Laird has shown to be groundless. That our powers of judgment are such that we can only doubt their competence to achieve certainty remains, however, as a reason for "total scepticism."

The question whether Hume is "one of those sceptics who hold that all is uncertain . . . is entirely superfluous," for neither Hume nor any other person has ever "constantly and sincerely" held that view.[183] Anyone who has been concerned "to refute the cavils of this *total* scepticism" has been trying to do by argument something already accomplished by nature. For "Nature, by an absolute and uncontrollable necessity has determined us to judge as well as to breathe and feel."[183] These natural judgments are the felt proofs and probabilities deriving from habits of inference, and they will carry comparative conviction in proportion to their force and vivacity. The Cartesians may well realize that if belief "were a simple act of thought," and not an operation of an habit of imagination, "it must infallibly destroy itself, and in every case terminate in a total suspense of judgment."[184] But that the arguments of the sceptics suffice to dethrone the reason of rationalistic philosophers does not mean that they extirpate habits of mind. And Hume's "intention . . . in displaying so carefully the arguments of that fantastic sect,"[183] is only to make it plain that the refutation of total scepticism is in truth his own view that reason consists of habits in imagination, and that belief is not "*cogitative*" but "*sensitive*" in nature.[183]

The sceptical arguments which Hume displays so carefully, describe inferences which are unnatural to the system of habits which is the understanding. That is why, although all "evidence" is of the nature of force and vivacity, we do not go through the self-destroying process described by members of the fantastic sect. For whenever in imagination we would run counter to these established customs, the action of the mind becomes forced and unnatural, and its ideas faint and obscure, with the result that we cannot long persist in any such course.[185]

Since it is only by this "singular and seemingly trivial property of the fancy"[268] that we avoid total scepticism, are we to conclude that all works of refined reasoning should be consigned to the flames? That would be a contradiction; for the reasoning of the *Treatise* itself "will be allowed to be sufficiently refined and metaphysical."[268] We would seem then to have to choose between a false reason and none at all. But, for that matter, if we would depend on reason conceived of as a mere act of the mind, we have seen that we should be left without conviction of any sort.[184] By the questions to which the empirical analysis of human nature gives rise, we would be then utterly confounded. "Most fortunately it happens, that since reason is incapable of dispelling these clouds, nature herself suffices to that purpose, and cures me of this philosophical melancholy and delirium...."[269] After a game of backgammon, such speculations on the incompetence of man as a rational animal appear "cold and strained and ridiculous."[269] But this means not that we return to our educated confidence in the pretensions of the

Cartesians, but that we accept the established habits of the mind as the one sound basis for all valid theory. "I may, nay I must yield to the current of nature, in submitting to my senses and understanding; and in this blind submission I show most perfectly my sceptical disposition and principles."[269] The sentiments of his spleen and indolence prompt Hume to ask why he should torture his brain with "subtleties and sophistries," in the absence of any prospect of attaining ever to truth and certainty. He answers that although philosophy be unable to discourage these sentiments in a man so disposed, he will nevertheless make bold to recommend its pursuit. For superstitions are easily acquired, and strongly influence the course of our inferences. "Philosophy on the contrary, if just, can present us only with mild and moderate sentiments; and if false and extravagant, its opinions are merely the objects of a cold and general speculation, and seldom go so far as to interrupt the course of our natural propensities."[272] The scepticism which we ought to maintain in "all the incidents of life"[270] is thus not "total" but "moderate." There are to be found "many honest gentlemen" whose imagination, being confined within the scope of daily affairs and conventional amusements, is not the stuff of which a truly philosophical understanding may be made. But if "we could communicate to our founders of systems a share of this gross earthy mixture, as an ingredient, which they commonly stand much in need of," Hume thinks that "we might hope to establish a system or set of opinions, which, if not true (for that, perhaps, is too much to be hoped for), might at least be satisfactory to the human mind, and might stand the test of the most critical examination."[272] Since the examination here would be experimental, and not that of metaphysical meditation, the prevalence of "chimerical systems" of philosophy which developed in the fancies of the ancient and modern philosophers is a fact irrelevant to the proper cultivation of that sensible philosophy, to whose advancement it is Hume's "only hope" that he may contribute "a little."*

Hume's scepticism with regard to reason is thus aimed at that total scepticism which would persuade us "that our judgment is not in *any* thing possessed of *any* measures of truth and falsehood."[183] If the arguments advanced by him for these sceptics prevail against such a

---

* "For my part, my only hope is, that I may contribute a little to the advancement of knowledge, by giving in some particulars a different turn to the speculations of philosophers, and pointing out to them more distinctly those subjects, where alone they can expect assurance and conviction. Human nature is the only science of man; and yet has been hitherto the most neglected."[273]

rationalism as that of "the Cartesians," they neither do nor could uproot those habits in imagination of which the more established constitute the understanding.[267] And in setting forth these arguments, Hume's intention, he tells us, is to make his readers the more sensible of the true view of reason, on which inference is not cogitative, but habitual in nature. This being the true view of reason, it is plain why "the sceptic still continues to reason and believe, even though he asserts, that he cannot defend his reason"[187] by a reason that can be not defended, but only denied, or ignored altogether, on a view of reason as an alleged faculty independent of imagination and custom.

Hume's theory of belief is sometimes referred to as though it were fully described in his statement that a belief is a lively idea associated with a present impression. That such is the case no one who has taken seriously Sections 8 to 14 of Book III will be likely to agree. The statement in question is no more than a definition of belief as distinguished from disbelief:[95] the full nature of belief is analysed in the subsequent six sections.

It is to be noticed, however, that in this initial description of belief, nothing more than the impressions, ideas, and associations into which Hume (in part) analyses the perceptions of the mind is involved. The ways in which ideas are associated with impressions are the ways in which we believe in perceived bodies or causes or our minds, or probabilities and chances. Therefore it would seem that, in this theory of belief taken as a whole, we have Hume's account of the different ways in which impressions and ideas are so related as to constitute various perceptions of the mind.

Considering the causes of belief, Hume finds them to be the three relations of association. But though ideas are found to be associated with impressions by resemblance, such beliefs are of the memory and senses alone. Moreover, that they may be beliefs in the existence of what is thus present, the associations cannot be of just any case of resemblance and contiguity. For there is "no manner of necessity" which could impel the mind to believe in the existence of perceptions thus constituted.[109] The Elysian fields of the young poet's imagination may in much detail resemble the meadows of Christ Church actually before him, but it would be only by "pure *caprice*"[109] that such a resemblance were formed in the fancy alone. Consequently, we must distinguish between the associations by resemblance of fancies with a present perception, and the associations within the perception in virtue of which it is a belief in the existence of what is thus present. These latter associations will be those resemblances and contiguities which are constant and coherent. For only those impressions and ideas which are intrinsically constant and coherent in their resemblance and contiguity are found to constitute the perceptions vulgarly called bodies.

Within the system of beliefs which is that of the memory and the senses alone, there are thus to be distinguished those beliefs which will be caused by just any association by resemblance and contiguity, and those caused only by such associations as are constant and coherent. Because these latter associations are repeated constantly, the habits thus formed will be very strong and concrete, or "entire." And as the perfect habits of causal inference have in their operations the felt force of proofs, so also the images supplied by these latter habits will have a force and vivacity indistinguishable from that of the sense-impressions by which they are evoked. Hence the association of such ideas with impressions will constitute a perception which believes in the existence of what it presents. On the other hand, "where upon the appearance of an impression we not only feign another object, but likewise arbitrarily, and of our mere goodwill and pleasure give it a particular relation to the impression, this can have but a small effect upon the mind;

nor is there any reason why, upon the return of the same impression, we should be determined to place the same object in the same relation to it."[109] The mind is not so determined, because the situation in question is not habitual in nature. Associations by resemblance or contiguity which are not determined by habit, but are fortuitous, have not the force of belief proper.[109] Thus, not every case of the association of a lively idea with a present impression is a belief in "real existence." That such may be the case, it is requisite that the association be not a matter of "pure *caprice*,"[109] but in virtue of an established habit.

The habit, however, need not be one of association by resemblance or contiguity. Though fortuitous associations are "very feeble and uncertain" in their influence, when the natural relation of cause and effect also is involved, the result will be a belief in real existence.[109] Moreover, when in belief the existence of something expected is inferred from something felt as actual, we then pass from the system of the memory and senses to that of judgment. The beliefs, which habitual associations by resemblance and contiguity alone contribute to constitute, will be beliefs in the "real existence" of things present. Only in cases where the natural relation of causation is involved will the belief be felt as transitive or inferential; and it is such beliefs as these that "people the world."

There are then two systems of habit which cause beliefs in the real (as distinguished from probable or possible) existence of the contents of the belief. These are, on the one hand, the habits that ground the beliefs in continued and independent existences, and, on the other, those customs which are the habits of causal inference felt as proofs. Within the beliefs thus grounded there are no constituents other than the impressions, ideas and natural relations into which (with recollections and fancies) Hume analyses the perceptions of the mind. Beliefs in real existence thus are so far seen to be identical with those perceptions of the mind which such beliefs are. And beliefs which are felt not as proofs but as probabilities will be found likewise to consist of these elements of perceptions.

Chance, being the name not of an ingredient of any belief, but of the absence of all association with the natural relation of cause and effect, is not a constituent of felt probabilities. This is true also of the number of chances in virtue of which one probability will be felt as superior to another. The three causes of the felt probability of chance, according to Hume, we have seen to be: (1) the habits of causal inference in virtue of which the die is expected to fall on one

side or another; (2) the "division" of this expectation equally over the several surfaces of the die;
(3) the "reuniting" of these six equal amounts
of impulses in the proportion of four to two.
The assumption on which this analysis is based
would seem to be the same as that underlying
the theory of philosophical relations. Since the
surfaces of the die are, as surfaces, not different
in quality or character, they are therefore at
once identical in quality and different in number.
The surfaces as such will therefore be felt indifferently; or, in Hume's language, the initial
expectation will be divided equally over the six
surfaces. In the next stage in Hume's analysis
here the same assumption is made. Four and two
respectively of the markings of the die being
identical in character, four impulses of expectation
will reunite on *any* one of the four numerically
different but qualitatively identical markings,
while the other two impulses will unite on *either*
of the two markings which remain.

In his analysis of the probability of chances
Hume introduces nothing alien to his theory of
relations. On the assumption (or the finding) that
resemblance is not a qualifying predicate, it will
follow that the surfaces *as such* will be qualitatively
identical as surfaces, and that the four sets of
pips will be likewise identical in character. In
view of the absence of difference in the surfaces

197

they will be felt indifferently or with equal amounts of expectation. This will be true also of any one of the four identical sets of pips, and of either of the other two sets. Since it is by this absence of difference in the surfaces of the four and two sets of pips respectively that the initial division and subsequent reunion of the impulse of expectation is explained, Hume's account of the origin of a felt superiority in chances involves nothing beyond intrinsically resembling impressions and ideas, and the natural relation of cause and effect.

A belief that the probability of chance A is superior to that of chance B will thus involve: (1) the habits of causal inference associated with the throwing of the die, (2) its perceived surfaces, (3) the four qualitatively identical sets of pips any one of which is chance A, and (4) the two identical sets of pips, either one of which is chance B. The felt superiority of chance A will arise not from a property of any A, but rather from the absence of difference among the four A's by which four units of the initially divided impulses are allowed to converge on any one A.

In all cases of those causal inferences distinguished as proofs it is plain that no more than the impressions, ideas, and habits of association which constitute the perceptions of the mind are involved. The analysis given of belief in the probability of causes is so far the same as that already given of the probability of chances that Hume feels under no obligation to take the matter any deeper.[135] In this connection, however, it is again to be noticed that the probability in question is not a property of any or all of the contents of a belief in the probability of causes. In all such cases the various ideas involved will be images not of impressions whose recurrence is uniform and constant, but rather of contrary impressions. Because all these contrary images are, as merely different, so many chances, the impulse of expectation characteristic of habits of causal inference will be initially divided equally among the various ideas. These amounts of impulse will then reunite on any one of a set of ideas among which there is a felt absence of difference. If ten ideas are resembling in being A, while eight are so in being B, the felt probability of the occurrence of the cause of A will be stronger than that of the probability of the cause of B. And when we compare the two beliefs, we will consider the first as a probability, the second as a possibility.

It has already been pointed out that, "Every past experiment may be considered as a kind of chance."[135] This would be to take the experiment as devoid of relations to all habits of association other than those internal to its constitution as a present perception. Bare chances would be either ideas merely entertained, or states of shock oblivious of all else; for chance as such is the negation of all causal associations. "The probabilities of causes are of several kinds; but are all derived from the same origin, viz. *the association of ideas to a present impression.* As the habit, which produces the association, arises from the frequent conjunction of objects, it must arrive at its perfection by degrees, and must acquire new force from each instance, that falls under our observation."[130] In mature persons the habits grounding their beliefs will be more or less fully formed, so that in their experience nothing corresponding to the gradation from probabilities to proofs is to be found. In ordinary experience what we have are beliefs of which we are conscious as a whole. The synthesis in belief, that is to say, is what is given; not isolated impressions, ideas, and associations, out of which and *after the fact of their being thus given*, we would formulate beliefs.

This is not to ignore the true importance for Hume's method of his "first principle"; it is only to suggest that his theory of belief be regarded as the analysis of the actual synthesis in which impressions, ideas, and associations ordinarily exist. Those terms are indeed among the ultimates of his analysis of the perceptions of the mind; and hence together they constitute the first principle of his method. Although that principle is unnecessary to his sceptical analysis of causation and personal identity, those terms do exhaust the contents of beliefs, whether they be probable or proofs. But in Hume's exposition of the nature of belief there would seem to be nothing to suggest that in his view, impressions, ideas, and associations in isolation come first in our actual experience, afterwards to be made consciously into beliefs. On the contrary, he points out that the development of proofs out of mere probabilities is usually insensible; that it is in the "remote degrees" of both that either may be perceived alone; and that probability as such—the felt indifference to all causes—is nothing which anyone "who is arrived at the age of maturity can any longer be acquainted with."[131] It is hence only in the extremes of disassociation that states of consciousness which express nothing may be found; the actual experience of mature persons will consist of beliefs and more or less unassociated fancies.

Experience for Hume is, then, in his own sense of the term, relational. Philosophical relations are to be sure not connections at all. But the natural relations of association are connections, and are so described by Hume.* They are also

* *Of the connection or association of ideas.*[10]

described as "principles of union or cohesion."[12] And he does not say that the source of order in the imagination superimposes itself on isolated impressions and ideas. It is rather that the perceptions of the mind are to be analysed into the impressions, ideas, and associations which are their *elements*. That Hume attempts by this analysis to exhibit the elements of the synthesis which is a perception is then not questioned when it is said that he also makes out at length the nature of this synthesis as such in his theory of belief. The analyses of Part I are thus properly viewed in the synthesis made out in Part III; a view in which it is seen that the one can be no more basic for Hume's theory of the understanding than the other.

Hume, like Locke, attaches great importance to the notion of composition. To analyse a perception would mean exhibiting its simple components. And Hume plainly views the fruits of his own analysis of perception with much satisfaction. It enables him to restore "idea" to its proper use, expeditiously to decide the metaphysical question of innate ideas, and yields him a principle of inquisition by which vested illusions as well as vulgar confusions in such matters as causation, substance, and belief may be disclosed. This satisfaction, together with a carelessness that is sometimes almost perverse in the use of "object" for "impression," "impression" for "object," and "perception" for either or both, may explain why, by the reiteration and the loose use of its terms, Hume's principle is made to seem little less than the substance of his theory of the understanding. For, because he thinks that nothing more important for deciding all disputes of however refined a nature has before been discovered, he gives those terms of his analysis a prominence in isolation that his theory of belief shows to be spurious.

This may explain why it is sometimes thought sufficient to make out Hume's scepticism as deriving exclusively from his principle that a simple idea must be the copy of a corresponding impression. Failing to find an impression of necessary connection, he denies that we have any such idea. This misses not only the actual conclusion of Hume's critical analysis of causation, but also his arguments to that conclusion from the impotence of apagogic reasoning in the matter, as well as the analytic efficacy of the further principle that what is distinguishable is separable; in effect, the substance of Hume's position in this regard. Again, although he does argue from the absence of any impression of substance to a denial of the idea, Hume also argues to that denial on the ground that the reality of the idea cannot be demonstrated by inference from the law of causation. And he advances an explanation of how it is that, in default of a copy of substance, we yet have beliefs in things as continuants.

Despite the priority in emphasis which Hume gives his doctrine of impressions and ideas, this dogma is not the single principle of his critique of the beliefs of human nature and the pretensions of philosophy. For also there is the assumption that what is distinguishable is separable, and there are the arguments regarding causation and substance which show the impotence of apagogic reasoning in matters of fact. This assumption is, as Mr. Laird has said, "almost ubiquitous in Hume's exposition."* And, by those arguments, Hume establishes a scepticism with regard to rationalism to which his "first principle" contributes nothing solid at all.

Since our beliefs in things as continued and independent existences are "entirely owing to the Imagination,"[193] it is to be expected that these beliefs also should consist exclusively of impressions and ideas in association. But that such is the case is not altogether clear. For the twofold characteristic of the contents of such beliefs is the constancy of their repetition and the constancy of their conjunction. Hume does make plain his opinion that the constancy with which

* John Laird, *Hume's Philosophy of Human Nature*, p. 82.

a perception is repeated is no more a distinguishable quality of the perception than is its being repeated at all. With respect to the term coherence, however, Hume's position is not so clear. Since the list of relations Hume gives is advanced as the exhaustive result of diligent consideration,[14] "coherence" is not the name of a relation. And it is evidently not the name of any impression. Either then the regular ways in which certain impressions and ideas vary with respect to one another, are as such "respects" which qualify those impressions and ideas, or these ways are simply the impressions and ideas themselves intrinsically so ordered in their occurrence. Beyond the fact that the second of these two alternatives is consistent with Hume's treatment of philosophical relations, while the first is not, there would seem to be no indication of what might be his view in the matter.

This difficulty being waived, however, we may notice that as beliefs in causes and effects consist exhaustively of impressions and ideas in their habits of association, so beliefs in things also are likewise constituted. A perception of the mind, then, taken as a whole, will consist not of an impression or of an idea, or of an association without terms, but of the synthesis in imagination which is a belief. A perception, that is to say, is the expression called a belief. Since, in the experience of mature persons, the development of their beliefs is a *fait accompli*, mature experience other than that of mere fancy will consist not of a succession of discrete impressions related to nothing beyond themselves, but rather of perceptions. Each perception will be the synthesis in habit of the impressions and ideas which constitute that particular belief. And those perceptions which are among themselves related by the natural relation of cause and effect will be the perceptual constituents of what Hume says is the true nature of the mind.

Within the system of causal beliefs which is the mind as thus defined, felt probabilities will distinguish themselves from felt proofs. The latter will constitute "the understanding, that is, . . . the general and more established properties of the imagination,"[267] in the sense that felt probabilities are less firmly established in habit than are proofs. Speaking of the habits in imagination which make us "reason from causes and effects," Hume says that "it is the same principle, which convinces us of the continued existence of external objects, when absent from the senses;" and he describes "these two operations" as being "equally natural and necessary in the human mind. . . ."[266] Within the established habits of imagination which constitute the understanding, Hume thus includes our everyday habits of belief in the continued and independent existence of everyday things.

In a lengthy footnote,[117, 118] Hume says that the term imagination is commonly used in two different senses; viz. that in which it refers to "the faculty, by which we form our fainter ideas," and a "larger" sense, not here defined. But Hume does here admit that often he has been loose in his use of the term imagination, and he concludes this footnote with the explanation that when he uses the term imagination as opposed neither to memory nor to reason, "it is indifferent whether it be taken in the larger or more limited sense, or at least the context will sufficiently explain the meaning." What this larger sense of the term is, Hume tells us explicitly not before the conclusion of his book on the understanding. "The memory, senses, and understanding are, therefore, all of them founded on the imagination, or the vivacity of our ideas."[265] In the larger sense, imagination is the generic name for the contents of consciousness.

The images of the senses and the impressions of reflection are not less but more sensuous than their copies preserved by the powers of association and recollection. Again, images recollected and fancies also are in and of imagination in the larger sense; and the natural relations are "the principles of union and cohesion" in imagination proper. Hume says above, "imagination *or* the force and vivacity of our ideas," because imagination, in this comprehensive sense, is sensuous force and vivacity explicit in imagery.

Although past experience recalled "is a principle which instructs me in the several conjunctions of objects"; and although "habit is another principle, which determines me to expect the same for the future," it is only because these principles so "conspire" as to "make me form certain ideas in a more intense and lively manner, than others," that Hume or any man can believe one argument rather than another, or extend his consciousness beyond the prospect of the present moment.[265] Without the effects of this conspiracy of experience recollected with habits of expectation, Hume would be unable to feign the continued and independent existence of any of his perceptions, and his consciousness thus would be reduced to that succession of causally related perceptions which constitutes his personal identity. But more than this, "even with relation to that succession, we could only admit of those perceptions which are immediately present to our consciousness, nor could those lively images, with which the memory presents us, be ever

received as true pictures of past perceptions."[265]
Were our experience fully described as a succession of perceptions, unrelated by the natural relation of cause and effect, it would be a succession in which each perception was oblivious of those past. Again, were the habits of imagination all equally forceful, that one belief should be stronger than another would be inexplicable. It is because imagination, although controlled by habit, is creative of perceptions varying in force and vivacity, that the two principles of constant conjunction and expectation can so conspire as to produce in imagination fictions of continued and independent existence, and beliefs ranging in the force of their contents from felt probabilities to felt proofs.

If describing Hume's theory of the understanding as a sensory phenomenalism places the emphasis as does Hume throughout the *Treatise*, it also tends to obscure the fact that, in his conclusion, Hume finds the imagination to be the foundation of the senses, as well as of the memory and understanding. His ambition to do for our knowledge of human nature what Newton had done for physics hardly requires mention. His debt to Locke and Berkeley has perhaps been largely repaid by those of his critics who would make Hume a synonym for his major mistake in principle. That Hume's "first principle," and so his method in philosophy, derives from the empiricism, and the atomism in psychology, of his two immediate British predecessors, is a view of the matter which, if perhaps *simpliste*, could hardly be termed false altogether. And Hume's scepticism regarding our presumed knowledge of bodies may derive wholly from Berkeley; though in this connection also he may be indebted to Malebranche, as is Berkeley himself in the opinion of recent students of the question.* But by his reference to the *XVe Éclaircissement* wherein Malebranche argues to the conclusion that logical connections are not to be found in matters of fact, Hume points it out that the sceptical analysis of causation which he expounds by his empirical method

* See R. I. Aaron, *Locke and Berkeley's Commonplace Book, Mind,* XL, N.S., 1931, pp. 439 sqq. (cf. Professor G. Dawes Hicks, *Berkeley,* p. 230). A. A. Luce, *Berkeley and Malebranche,* Oxford Press, 1934. Dr. Luce's treatment of his subject raises questions of interpretation, particularly with regard to Malebranche, that seem to me seriously to weaken the force of his main case. Nevertheless, much of the evidence adduced by him strongly suggests the need for a further reconsideration of the current view in which the development of British Empiricism is regarded as a self-contained growth. If, and in so far as, Berkeley's immaterialism be derived from Malebranche's arguments against any direct knowledge of matter itself, and in so far as Hume's sceptical position in that regard derives from Berkeley's denial of matter altogether, there would then be that further case of Malebranche's influence on the development of British Empiricism. Yet, even though so much were established, it would not follow that Hume's theory of belief in substance is (or could be) an inference from Berkeley's several reasons for denying the existence of matter.

derives from no empiricism, but from a rationalism which, by its critique of efficient causation,
in effect denies its own pretensions to *a priori*
knowledge in matters of fact. This was concealed
from Malebranche by his theory of knowledge
as the vision in God. But to one acquainted with
the total scepticism of the fantastic sect, it meant
that the reason of the Cartesians could be
defended by an appeal neither to that alleged
reason itself nor to the experience of the senses.
For nowhere in experience is logical necessity
holding between individuals to be found. The
pretensions of the Cartesians to an understanding
of nature by reason must then be groundless
and their very method mistaken. Since neither
reason nor the senses can support the edifice of
human belief, the imagination alone remains.
To show that this is so, Hume exposes the
impotence of apagogic reasoning in all matters
concerning causation, as well as the futility of
reasoning from the law of causation to the
existence of substance; and by the use of his
"first principle" he displays the inadequacy of a
purely sensory phenomenalism to the questions
at issue, thus making it plain that the foundation
of the understanding is imagination. That he
argues to this final end by a method mistaken
in principle can hardly affect either the truth of
the conclusion that the contradictory of no

inference about matters of fact is inconceivable, or the further fact that his sceptical conclusions regarding causation and personal identity are to be found in the writings of some of the Cartesians.

It would then be well to distinguish this truth and these conclusions from the empirical and atomistic method by which Hume sought to establish them. And since the disclosed failure, both of reason and the senses, to support the pretensions of our beliefs in causation and substance, constitutes the critical part of Hume's theory of the understanding, it may be well that this part should be firmly distinguished from his constructive theory, which is that of belief as the synthesis *in* imagination of those elements *of* imagination which exclude mere fancies or "perfect" ideas.

Hume gives us no general rules by which to distinguish between hallucinations and real existences. Indeed, in the section on the impressions of the memory and the senses he as much as denies that in any given case such a distinction could be established. He does, however, give us rules by which to judge of causes and effects; and he does so with the express intention of meeting the objection that, within his system, no practical distinction may be made between the unphilosophical probabilities of popular credence and the proofs and probabilities of sound belief. "According to my system," he says, "all reasonings are nothing but the effects of custom; and custom has no influence, but by enlivening the imagination, and giving us a strong conception of any object. It may, therefore, be concluded, that our judgment and imagination can never be contrary, and that custom cannot operate on the latter faculty after such a manner as to render it opposite to the former."[149] Since the felt force of imagination is the deciding factor in belief, what can it mean to say that we ought to reject the unphilosophical though strongly felt probabilities of popular belief, and accept the less strongly felt probabilities engendered in imagination by the study of the experimental sciences? Hume answers frankly, "This difficulty we can remove after no other manner than by supposing the influence of general rules."[149] The rules in question are those by which we ought to regulate our judgment concerning causes and effects; "and these rules are formed on the nature of our understanding, and on our experience of its operations in the judgments we form concerning objects."[149] It is thus plain that Hume takes his rules governing causal inference to be an analysis of the nature of our understanding in so far as it consists of habits of causal inference. Hence, the imagination which is "the ultimate judge of all systems of philosophy,"[225] is neither that of popular opinion nor that of scholarship in ancient philosophy, but rather that within which an understanding has been engendered by the experimental observation of causes and effects.

Of Hume's eight rules the first three are definitions which together again define the relation of cause and effect. In his fourth rule he in effect denies both plurality of causes and plurality of effects. In the course of so doing he explains again how it is that a cause or an effect is inferred from a single experience of its correlative. "For when by any clear experiment we have discovered the causes or effects of any phenomenon, we immediately extend our observation to every phenomenon of the same kind, without waiting for that constant repetition, from which the first idea of this relation is derived."[173, 174] Since it is by the constant repetition of conjoined events that habits of causal inference are produced, upon the recurrence of a perception called cause the idea of its constant conjunct will be evoked in imagination in virtue of the habit of which that idea is a constituent. Consequently, upon the occurrence of an unfamiliar event which in any respect resembles a familiar cause or effect, the unfamiliar event will be associated by that resemblance with a habit of causal inference which will serve to give force to the inference from that event to an imagined conjunct.

In his fifth and sixth rules Hume deduces from the fourth that any similarity among effects must be due to a common quality in the cause; and that, where there is any difference among effects there must be some difference in their cause. His seventh rule explains that where there is concomitant variation in causes and their effects, it must be supposed that these perceptions are composed of several different causes and effects whose presence or absence varies with the ascertained concomitance. The eighth and last rule explains that whenever a cause is fully present, and the effect is absent, this cause is not the sole cause of the effect in question.[173-4]

It will be by understanding these definitions and practising these methods of experiment that "we learn to distinguish the accidental circumstances from the efficacious causes."[149] When, by experiment, we find that an effect can be produced in the absence of a suspected cause, we conclude that such is not the cause sought for,[149] but an accidental circumstance, frequently conjoined with the perception in question.[149] "But as this frequent conjunction necessarily makes it have some effect on the imagination," there is a conflict between the slight habit thus formed and the general rule or "judgment."

This conflict is resolved when we attribute "the one inference" to our fancy, the other to our judgment or understanding.[149] Such accidental coincidences and analogies may, however, engender habits which will become firmly established in careless minds. "Thus our general rules are in a manner set in opposition to each other."[149] But whenever we consider any such act of the imagination, "and compare it with the more general and authentic operations of the understanding, we find it to be of an irregular nature, and destructive of all the most established principles of reasoning; which is the cause of our rejecting it."[150] Though general rules or judgments of the former sort commonly prevail among the vulgar, wise men will be guided by an understanding engendered by experiment in accordance with these rules.

If it is too much to say of these "permanent, irresistible, and universal" habits (or "principles") of imagination, as opposed to those "which are changeable, weak, and irregular," that they "are the foundation of all our thoughts and actions, so that upon their removal human nature must immediately perish and go to ruin,"[225] still Hume may well emphasize the conclusion that all of our beliefs that are justified by experimental enquiry and all of our accurately successful causal inferences will depend upon the operation in the understanding of those fundamental habits by which cases of constant conjunction are disclosed and inferred. The nature of the understanding thus is what constitutes the foundations of induction. That the habits of which the understanding consists can in no case yield demonstrably certain conclusions, means that the foundations of induction are essentially alogical, to be neither demonstrated nor denied either by the reason of the Cartesians or by inductive theory itself. It is, finally, of the nature of the understanding that logic proper consists: the pretensions of "our scholastic headpieces and logicians" are simply to be set aside.[175]

APPENDIX

On Hume's Atomism in Philosophy

THE five major assumptions of Hume's epistemology would seem to be (1) that experience may be exhaustively analysed into elements; (2) that every simple idea is the copy of a simple impression; (3) that resemblance and difference (taken "philosophically") are neither qualifying predicates nor relations; (4) that what is distinguishable is separable; and (5) the attraction of association.

Of these five assumptions, the second and fifth state the main content of the first, while the third and fourth would seem to express Hume's own view of his so-called atomism in philosophy. For Hume held that the elements of experience are not connected in virtue of their being qualitatively identical or different. Consequently wherever there is a difference among experiences, an actual separation, as in the case of a mere fancy, may occur. Thus in principle, any discriminable experience may be separated without alteration from any other such. This is the case because, on this view, the identity of any single experience is intrinsic, not relative to anything lying beyond the experience itself. For "resemblance" is assumed to mean what is meant by a qualitative identity numerically distributed, where qualitative identity is intrinsic or absolute, not relative, and difference indicates the "negation"[15] of resemblance. Since the elements of experience are thus intrinsically self-identical, and cases of resemblance are precisely the qualitatively identical cases themselves, those elements are self-contained. Therefore any complex may be analysed into its elements without remainder, and

218

without the elements thereby being altered. Where there is a distinction a separation may occur for the reason that what is thus distinct is intrinsically self-identical because neither resemblance nor difference are qualifying predicates. In virtue of its intrinsic identity, no element can be altered; and since resembling elements are simply the qualitatively identical elements themselves, no analysis of a complex can either alter, or find anything over and above, the elements of the complex analysed.

It would thus be crudely unfair to maintain that Hume's view of the constitution of experience is the result of an entirely uncritical acceptance of the composition theory of his British predecessors. For by his theory of philosophical relations, and his explanatory analysis of the meaning of "resemblance" and "being simple," Hume would seem to have indicated the main logical presupposition of his dictum that what is distinguishable is separable. Since neither "resemblance" nor "difference" name qualifying predicates or natures or forms of any sort, by which resembling or different elements are in any sense connected, where there is a distinction there can be no *reason* (the contradictory of which would be inconceivable) why a separation should not there occur. Hume's "atomism," then, is in principle the assumption that whatever is distinguishable is intrinsically self-identical, and therefore self-contained.

To reject this assumption because, as made by Hume, it derives from an inadequate analysis of relations of comparison, is one thing; and to reject the analyses of experience that Hume does make on the ground that they are "atomistic" is, it would seem, another. In the latter case, the rejection springs from grounds that are incompatible with Hume's theory of philosophical relations. It is fortunately not necessary to attempt to circumscribe these grounds, even summarily. They would be sufficiently illustrated by any view of experience as a systematic whole, by the view (or views) of relations as internal, and by the thesis that experiences exist not in succession but in process.

On the view that experience is a systematic whole the character of any experience will be in some sense determined by its systematic relations within the whole: hence no experience could be intrinsically self-identical and self-contained. Hume refers to the "realities" that are perceived bodies, and to the "realities" that are in part inferred causes or effects as "systems"; and, in an early letter, he speaks of his philosophy itself as a system.* But within these systems it is assumed that the elements do not determine the character of the whole, or belief, which they do exhaustively constitute.

Hume's "systems" thus are not systematic; they are not of the nature of an organic whole: rather, they are syntheses or combinations of intrinsically individuated elements that appear in association. Since Hume finds association to be a distinguishable constituent of the synthesis that is a belief, association is therefore a separable element of perception. The gentle force that is the defining characteristic of the natural relations thus is external to the terms it "unites" in the sense that it does not "penetrate and alter" or "make a difference" in its terms. The principle of union within the understanding is thus external to the terms it associates.

We have noticed that, on Hume's view of the meaning of the term existence, it is difficult to understand how the constituents of perception can be repeatable. It is no less difficult to see how the terms "development" and

* *The Letters of David Hume*, J. Y. T. Greig, letter 6. See above, p. 213.

Appendix

"process" can have meaning for Hume. He plainly holds perceptions and their contents to be successive merely. Hence no questions as to the nature of development, and thus no questions as to the reality of universals as species, arise to conflict with the theory of abstract ideas which he considers adequate. Taking Hume's view of the successive contents of perception *au pied de la lettre*, we can only conclude that cases of the gentle force simply occur.

Since distinguishable perceptions are separable, they may detach themselves from the system of perceptions that is the mind, and their independent existence is thus conceivable. But if perceptions are separable, why not ideas, impressions, and cases of the gentle force? They are distinguishable, and therefore must be separable. Consistently with Hume's dictum, that this is conceivable can only be admitted. Hume finds in fact that mere fancies do so occur; and we have noticed that such would be the case were a mere chance to exist. To say that the elements of perception might occur in utter isolation is thus to make a statement of which the contradictory is not inconceivable on the basis of Hume's dictum. But it is important to notice that what such a statement would be about is, in Hume's terms, always a bare chance.

Nevertheless it may be urged, the question remains: is a relation such as association conceivable as separate and without terms? On the assumed validity of Hume's dictum, the answer, we have noticed, must be affirmative. But that there may not be terms without relations, and relations without terms, is perhaps the principle of the main lines of objection against Hume's logical atomism. For if Hume's dictum is true, experience cannot be systemic, and relations cannot be internal. Moreover since these terms and relations are separable in virtue of their being intrinsically individuated and self-contained, it is difficult to see how they could be in process.

In order then that the force of this line of criticism may be indicated, it may be well that, at the risk of seeming irrelevance, brief reference should be made to Bradley's argument for the internality of relations.

In Chapter III of *Appearance and Reality*, it is argued that qualities imply relations; and relations in the sense that they alone differentiate qualities. If this is true, it follows that any alteration in a relation (or differentiation) would imply a qualitative difference in its terms. Hence an internal relation is a relation that differentiates its terms. When the differentiation is altered, the terms are *ipso facto* altered.

Thus Bradley writes: "I rest my argument upon this, that if there are no differences, there are no qualities, since all must fall into one. But, if there is any difference, then that implies a relation. Without a relation it has no meaning; . . . And this is the point on which all seems to turn. Is it possible to think of qualities without thinking of distinct characters?"* Bradley's answer to this question is of course negative. That they may be many, qualities must be distinct; and this distinctness cannot be a difference that is numerical merely. "For consider, the qualities A and B are to be different from each other; and, if so, that difference must fall somewhere. If it falls, in any degree or to any extent, outside A or B, we have relation at once. But, on the other hand, how can difference and otherness fall inside? If we have in A any such otherness, then inside A we must distinguish its own quality and its otherness."† The difference, in virtue of

* *Appearance and Reality* (originally published by George Allen & Unwin, now published by the Oxford University Press) p. 29.
† Ibid.

which A is one of many qualities, cannot fall within the character of A; for were it within A, there then would be an infinite regress of differences within A itself. The difference, then, must fall outside A. On the assumption that "difference" is the name of a relation, this means that A, in virtue of its difference from other qualities, is by that very difference related to them.

As in Chapter II,* the alternative to relations that imply terms is an infinite regress in relations that do not relate, so, in Chapter III, the alternative to qualities differentiated by their relations is an infinite regress within quality. Therefore relations are internal to, i.e. implicated in, their terms; and terms are likewise internal to their relations. By the very fact of an alteration in the one there is alteration in the other. Hence the identity of no term or relation is absolute: identity implies difference; and, since difference here is a relation, identity therefore is relative.†

It will be recalled that Hume views difference as the negation of relation, and that the validity of his dictum depends on the assumption that neither resemblance nor

* *Appearance and Reality*, p. 21.

† Mr. Ewing, in his *Idealism*, pp. 130, 131, explains that the view on which relations are internal in the sense that they "make a difference to" their terms, "means that, where two terms are related in some specific way, it is always true that they could not both have been what they are without the relation being present. This is true, e.g. of most or all quantitative relations and of the relation of similarity or difference." On Hume's view, this would then be true of relations "such as depend entirely" on their terms. Thus it is the case (if it be useful to say so) that such relations are internal, in this general sense of the term. However, the self-identity of resembling content being for Hume absolute, not relative or contextual, it is hardly necessary to remark that his conception of philosophical relations is other than that with which Chapters II and III of *Appearance and Reality* are concerned.

difference are qualifying predicates. For only on that assumption may the distinct be separable without alteration. The validity of the dictum that what is distinguishable is separable thus requires that difference be the negation of relation, whereas in Bradley's view a difference is a relation implicated in the quality of the terms it differentiates. On the one assumption, experiences are intrinsically individuated and absolutely self-contained; on the other, the identity of qualities and relations is relative.

This issue may be sharpened by pointing out that on the view that relations are implicated in their terms, no relation and no term is repeatable. For *this* difference, and *these* qualities thus differentiated, are what they are in virtue of their context. As any alteration in the relation or terms is *ipso facto* an alteration in the context or systemic whole, just so any alteration in the context is an alteration in the terms and their relation. No pair of terms in this context can be the same in any other context. Hence it would be true not only that no case of association could occur in separation, but that neither impressions nor ideas could be repeated.

Difference, Hume says, "is of two kinds as opposed either to identity or resemblance. The first is called a difference of *number*; the other of *kind*."[15] He has explained that resemblance is not the name of a quality distinguishable from the elements of experience, and that abstract adjectives and class names refer to (by their association with) any one of the qualitatively identical contents of a habit in imagination. Different *kinds* thus are nominal, while the various qualitative identities to which the names refer are not nominal but rather concrete elements of experience. And these cases of qualitative identities, being in no sense related by a common, discriminable property or resemblance, are numerically different merely. Hume's assumption that elements of experience may and do recur is thus consistent with his theory of philosophical relations. On that theory, the difference between recurring resemblances is merely numerical, and the assumption that all difference is difference in quality is thus denied. Yet if Bradley's arguments concerning qualities and relations are final, Hume's theory of philosophical relations is to be rejected as a barren illusion. It would appear, however, that in assuming difference to be difference in quality, Bradley begs a large part of his conclusion here. Clearly, that they may be many, qualities must be in some sense different. This difference "must fall somewhere"; and it must fall either "inside" or "outside" A. The difference cannot fall inside A. For that would differentiate A within itself into A_1 and A_2; and, since this is a question of principle, A_1 and A_2 would be differentiated within themselves indefinitely. The difference must then fall "outside A"; and thus "we have relation at once." On the assumption that difference is a relation, these considerations would seem to rule out as inconceivable a plurality of undifferentiated and so unrelated qualities.

Yet the conclusion that different qualities must have relations that they may be differentiated, even as relations must have qualities that may be relations, is one thing; and the conclusion that any difference made in relations and terms can be only a difference that is qualitative, is another. For this conclusion follows from the first only on the assumption that all difference is difference in quality. Without that assumption, it might be the case that an alteration in a relation should entail a merely numerical difference in the terms. The new relation, that is to say, might be altered in character while the new terms would be numerically different from, but qualitatively identical with, the old. Thus, though it be plain that the idea of a relation without terms is a delusion, and though it be the case that qualities without relation are inconceivable, still, from these two conclusions it follows neither that any alteration in a relation must make a qualitative difference in its terms, nor that any change in a quality must make a qualitative difference in its relations. For from these conclusions this further contention follows only in virtue of a further premise; namely, that to be different is to be different in quality. Yet neither Bradley's exclusion of the alternative of separate relations, nor his exclusion of that of quality without relation, implies this third premise. It remains, therefore, an open alternative that some difference be numerical.* Hence the assumption of absolute identity and the repetition of qualitative identities numerically distributed has not been ruled out.

But if the assumption that difference is not a qualifying predicate and the dependent theory of philosophical relations are thus not shown to be impossible by the argument we have noticed above, the bearing of Hume's dictum, it is plain, has been restricted. Although Hume still may assume that resemblance and difference are not qualifying predicates, as well as the consequence of this that any complex may be analysed without remainder into its elements, he may no longer take it that wherever there is a distinction a blank separation may occur. For every relation, it would seem, requires some pair of terms or other, with the consequence that the occurrence of a case of association with no terms whatever is inconceivable.

* Whether or not this alternative is excluded by Bradley's theory of predication is, of course, a further question. Yet it may be remarked that the alleged dilemma of predication would appear to be such only on the assumption that predication is an internal relation. Cf. *Identity and Implication, Philosophical Review*, Vol. XLIII, No. 3.

Appendix

In an *Appendix* to the *Treatise*, which it may be well to quote at length, Hume himself asks for more in the way of a connection between the perceptions that constitute the self than he has been able to find. "If perceptions are distinct existences, they form a whole only by being connected together. But no connections among distinct existences are ever discoverable by human understanding. We only *feel* a connection or determination of the thought, to pass from one object to another. It follows therefore, that the thought alone finds personal identity, when reflecting on the train of past perceptions, that compose a mind, the ideas of them are felt to be connected together, and naturally introduce each other. However extraordinary this conclusion may seem, it need not surprise us. Most philosophers seem inclined to think that personal identity *arises* from consciousness; and consciousness is nothing but a reflected thought or perception. The present philosophy, therefore, has so far a promising aspect. But all my hopes vanish, when I come to explain the principles that unite our successive perceptions in our thought or consciousness. I cannot discover any theory which gives me satisfaction on this head.

"In short there are two principles which I cannot render consistent; nor is it in my power to renounce either of them, viz. *that all our distinct perceptions are distinct existences*, and *that the mind never perceives any real connection among distinct existences*. Did our perceptions either inhere in something simple and individual, or did the mind perceive some real connection among them, there would be no difficulty in the case."[635, 636] The only connections between distinct preceptions to be discovered are *felt* connections, viz. the felt determinations of habit. This conclusion may appear to be "extraordinary"; but, so far at least, Hume thinks his view of the matter "promising." It is when he comes to explain the principles of this felt union that his hopes vanish. For there are "two principles" which he can neither renounce nor reconcile, viz. that perceptions are distinct existences, and that among distinct existences no "real connections" are to be found.

Now what are these "real connections"? Are they cases of the gentle force? If so, Hume is here saying that what he constantly asserts throughout the *Treatise* as a matter of fact is in fact not to be found. Moreover he is denying the existence of what, in the immediately preceding paragraph, he says he does find, viz. "*felt* connections," or "determinations of the thought." It is, then, hardly likely that the "real connections" in question are cases of association. Yet it is plain that the explanation which Hume has given of the organization of the self no longer satisfies him. He now seeks more than the *felt* connection which he says we do find; he requires connections that will be in some sense "real." For did perceptions "inhere in something simple and individual," or were "some real connection among them" discoverable, "there would be no difficulty in the case." Thus real connections are what would be the satisfactory alternative here to a simple spiritual substance. And since this alternative is not the fact of the felt connections which we do find, what is required is a connection that would be "real" in some sense opposed to that of being merely felt. This suggests that the connections in question are the logical connections in experience which the Cartesians failed to discover. For such logical relations are among what Hume also fails to find throughout the course of his examination of experience.

Whatever Hume may have meant here by a real connection, it is the case that in thus explaining why he regards his constructive theory of the self as "very defective,"[635] Hume does not say that he rejects the best he has been able to do. The description of personal identity in terms of felt determinations or habitual connections of perceptions "has so far a promising aspect." This promise falls short of disclosing the real (as opposed to the merely felt) connection that unites the perceptions of the mind. Hence Hume pleads "the privilege of a sceptic." Were the requisite connection to be discovered, a statement of the "real" principle of personal identity might then replace the mere description of the facts that Hume could find.

Since Hume holds that "to explain it [personal identity] perfectly we must take the matter pretty deep, and account for that identity, which we attribute to plants and animals; there being a great analogy between it and the identity of a self or person."[253] presumably he would agree that what he now requires in the case of the individual person is, by "a great analogy," requisite to the individuality of any individual continuant. If the natural relations do not afford a sufficiently real principle of union in the self, this deficiency is no less present in Hume's account of the substantial identity of "plants and animals." A real connection, closely analogous to that necessary for a satisfactory account of personal identity, will then be required that the individuality of plants and animals may be properly accounted for. Yet, that Hume thus acknowledges his constructive theory of the self to be very defective plainly does not mean that he considers his view here to be worse than inadequate.

In view of the conclusion that every term requires some relation or other and that every relation requires some pair of terms or other, it cannot be the case that terms and relations are merely separable. But, even so, from this it does not follow that in a given case we know that neither the terms nor the relations could have been otherwise. Though the contradictory of the proposition that every relation requires some terms or other be inconceivable, the contradictory of the proposition "R requires A and B" remains conceivable. For from the conclusion that R must have some terms or other, what in particular those terms must be may not be inferred. Hence R might have A_2 and B_2 while remaining unaltered. To acknowledge that terms require relations and that relations require terms in so far to know only that: it is not to know, in any particular case, that there is a necessary connection between a particular relation and a certain pair of terms. It is, therefore, not known *a priori* that to change the relation in a given case is to change in quality the terms that existed before the change in the relation. The assumption that complexes may be analysed into their elements without the elements thereby being altered, thus is not ruled out by the conclusion that the possibility of isolated terms and relations is a delusion.

The fact that Hume's dictum implies that isolated terms and relations *may* occur, is not the fact that isolated impressions and ideas normally do so occur in his view. For the assumption that the syntheses that are beliefs or perceptions consist exhaustively of intrinsically individuated elements does not in fact carry with it the view that it is these elements that first appear in isolation, thereafter to be made into syntheses. Perceptions occur; and, on Hume's principles, they may be and are analysed into what he takes to be their elements. Did Hume's theory of the understanding consist only of the analysis of the perceptions of the mind that is Part I, and his critical analysis of certain beliefs about causation and substance, it might be suggested that for him experience is a succession of isolated elements. But nothing would be more unaccountable than the activity of the imagination which, in his conclusion, Hume finds to be the foundation of the senses and the memory, were it uncontrolled by any universal principles. The variety of habits in imagination which develop in virtue of the natural relations of association, Hume exhibits in the syntheses that are those habits by his elucidation of the nature of our beliefs in Part III of the *Treatise*. It is thus in the synthesis made out in Part III that the analysis of Part I is properly to be viewed. Thus regarded, the elements of perception are seen not as the terms of an analysis, but as the constituents of the systems that are the beliefs or perceptions of which experience unanalysed consists.

The constituents of this experience are "atomic" in the sense that their identity is not relative but intrinsic; a view of identity which, in this case, assumes that resemblance and difference are not qualifying predicates. An examination, as distinguished from a metaphorical baptism, of that one of Hume's major assumptions would then be a critique of his "atomism." To reject the doctrine of impressions and ideas as a theory in psychology that more than once has been shown to be unable to maintain its own distinctions, is not to indicate the assumptions in logic on which the intrinsic identity of those elements of perception depend. For though both the assumption that experience may be analysed into elements, and the arguments to the conclusion that such of these elements as are terms are intrinsically individuated ideas that can only be copies of self-contained impressions, require the theory of philosophical relations, the converse is not the case. That theory about relations of comparison, and the dictum that what is distinguishable is separable, require the assumption that "resemblance" and "difference" are not the names of common properties, or of "principles of union" of any sort. For it is in virtue of that assumption that Hume may take relations of comparison to be not relations at all, but rather numerically different terms, that are comparable because they are qualitatively identical. He may therefore assume perceptions to be analysable into elements, with no remainder of common properties or logical relations distinguishable from the elements themselves. This assumption that the elements of experience are intrinsically self-identical is thus requisite to the view of impressions as "complete in themselves." But the finding of elements by analysis is itself not the further explanation that these elements may be regarded as self-contained because, like "being simple," "resemblance" is not the name of a qualifying predicate.

Whether or not the theory of philosophical relations be rejected along with the doctrine of impressions and ideas, the conclusion, as such, that apagogic reasoning is powerless in matters of existence, remains no less independent of that theory and that doctrine, than is the conclusion itself of Hume's failure to find necessary connections among matters of fact. Although this failure had been anticipated in some detail by La Forge, Cordemoy, and Malebranche, it would be a mistake to suggest that Hume did no more than re-state their negative conclusions. For, as Professor Kemp Smith has pointed out, it was Hume who first perceived the falsity of the Cartesian, rationalistic view of the causal relation.* Malebranche could discover no necessary connection between events, yet he continued to conceive of the causal relation as being

* N. Kemp Smith, *A Commentary to Kant's Critique of Pure Reason*, p. 597.

intelligible to the pure understanding, and, as a consequence of his theory of knowledge as the vision in God, failed to draw the conclusion that the law of causation is neither intuitively nor demonstrably certain. This conclusion drawn, Hume can attack the root of any assumption that the law of causation may be justified by experience. The attempted justification could only be inductive; and the law of causation is the presupposition of induction. Since causal inference is found to be neither rational nor merely sensory, if explicable at all, it will be so through an analysis, not of the fancies of the philosophers, but of the imagination that is the foundation of the senses and the memory. It is thus found that probable inference consists of the habits of imagination, or beliefs, which are the perceptions that constitute the mind, and of which the more firmly established in the imagination are the understanding.

INDEX

235

Index

237